NUMEROLOGY

NUMEROLOGY
Austin Coates

*It is easier to move a mountain
than alter a person's character
—Chinese Proverb*

THE CITADEL PRESS   SECAUCUS, N.J.

First American edition, 1975
Copyright © 1974 by Austin Coates
All rights reserved
Published by Citadel Press
A division of Lyle Stuart, Inc.
120 Enterprise Ave., Secaucus, N.J. 07094
First published in the United Kingdom by
Frederick Muller Limited
Manufactured in the United States of America

ISBN 0-8065-0497-8 (clothbound)
ISBN 0-8065-0499-4 (paperbound)

Lithographed in the U.S.A.
by Noble Offset Printers, Inc.
New York, N.Y. 10003

NUMEROLOGY is described in many a dictionary as the study of the occult significance of numbers. Occult means hidden.

To me as a child, arithmetic was hidden, because I could not do it correctly, except by accident.

Grown up, I had to read statistics. Sometimes these concerned entire populations, the charts being so large and complex that they covered the entire wall of a room.

It was there I learned that exposure to numbers on this scale confounds most men, however quick they may be at arithmetic.

To a great majority, statistics are occult. Most people understand only what the statistician explains by word and graph. They do not perceive the message of the numbers themselves, unless these are explained.

Numerology is another branch of knowledge to which the same applies. Once you understand it, there is—*pace* the dictionaries—nothing occult about it.

Statistics speak, if by looking at them you can hear what they are saying.

The same is true of numerology. The word means the speech of numbers.

CONTENTS

To
Tan Kok Seng
and
Esmée Daw Thin Mya
who encouraged
from opposite sides
of the world

This book explains an inner principle of numerals in relation to human personality.

The most ancient utterance of the mind of man is a statement of numerology, inscribed on the back of a tortoise in China—the Eight Trigrams.

I have studied numerology for forty years, since I was eleven.

Never having heard of the Eight Trigrams when I started (in London), I came to realize that the principle which I discerned from experience of numerals accorded with the inscription on the tortoise's back.

AUSTIN COATES

I

A LOCKED DOOR IN DARKNESS

I

The Key

In order to understand the meaning of the nine numerals in relation to human personality, they have to be set out as a grid, thus:

$$3 \quad 6 \quad 9$$

$$2 \quad 5 \quad 8$$

$$1 \quad 4 \quad 7$$

In this form, they are divided into six principal lines, three vertical and three horizontal.

Taking the vertical lines first, the line 3, 2, 1 consists of numbers of thought, connected with the element of air. The line 6, 5, 4 consists of numbers of activity, connected with the element of earth. The line 9, 8, 7 consists of numbers of power, connected with the heaviest of the elements, water.

Needless to say, there is no actual connection between numbers and elements. It is simply that associating the two provides a convenient method of explaining certain aspects of numbers.

The horizontal lines have first to be considered in relation to the human body. The top line, 3, 6, 9, consists of numbers of the head. The middle line, 2, 5, 8, consists of numbers of the heart. The bottom line, 1, 4, 7, consists of numbers of the stomach.

Next, the same three lines need to be seen in relation to a country landscape with crops. The top line, 3, 6, 9, represents sunlight (and rain), without which the crops will not grow. The middle line, 2, 5, 8, represents the crop itself,

3

the produce of the earth. The bottom line, 1, 4, 7, represents the soil, out of which the produce arises.

Combining the vertical and horizontal meanings gives this diagram:

		Thought Air	Activity Earth	Power Water
Sunlight	Head	3	6	9
Produce	Heart	2	5	8
Soil	Stomach	1	4	7

This diagram is the key to the meaning of numbers, and is the basis of numerology.

After observing it carefully for some time, it will be found that it begins to explain itself. The following is a rudimentary analysis of it as it stands.

In ONE the earthy stomach stands in conjunction with airy thought. This is a strong, healthy mixture, the world on a fine day. ONE being attached to the earth, airy thought is moored and practical, concerned with human realities. This is the number of invention and literature.

In TWO the productive heart is conjoined with airy thought. This is a more difficult proposition. The heart being what it is, whether productive or not, it may, not being moored to earth, prove to be the kite that flies away. This is a number of emotion, desire and imagination.

In THREE the sunlit head is in conjunction with airy thought, each in its natural element, causing this to be a number of happiness, ease, and fulfilled self-expression in the general realm of thought.

In FOUR the earthy stomach conjoins with earthy activity, suggestive of much activity in a defined sphere, turning over the same soil again and again, and thus, if carried to excess, much ado about nothing.

In FIVE the productive heart stands in conjunction with earthy activity, a healthy combination, in which the heart directs itself to the practical and necessary. This is the number of industry, politics and general organization, both civil and military.

In SIX the sunlit head is in conjunction with earthy activity. The head, full of ideas, here applies itself to the activities of the earth. This is the number of commerce, enterprise and law.

In SEVEN the earthy stomach lies conjoined with watery power, a situation liable to end in mud. This is the number of agriculture: human power applied to the soil.

In EIGHT the productive heart beats in conjunction with watery power, which has a steadying and sobering effect on the heart, causing it to engage in steady pursuits, at the root of which is trust. It is the number of banking, insurance and shipping: human power applied to productive matters which are not necessarily tied to the soil.

In NINE the sunlit head beats on watery power, resulting in heat. Heat *qua* heat is virtually useless. Applied to something, it becomes the most powerful of forces. This is the number of sheer power, which must be applied or harnessed to something in order to become useful. It is also the number of money which, by the same tokens, when applied to a transaction, acquires merit.

Observe the grid again:

3	6	9
2	5	8
1	4	7

Taking the vertical lines first:

3, 2, 1, being numbers of thought and air, are individualists. They take uneasily to combining with others. ONE finds combination virtually impossible. TWO, with self-control, can sometimes manage it, though seldom for long, whilst THREE, which is the number of combination (1 and 2), finds combination difficult, unless as a leader, when he is at ease.

6, 5, 4, numbers of activity and earth, are organizers of material things. FOUR, turning over the same earth again and again, is the organizer of detail. FIVE, the politician, is the general organizer and co-ordinator and also represents industry. SIX, the man of commerce, organizes in respect of goods and money.

9, 8, 7, numbers of power and water, are influencers. NINE, being (horizontally) a head number, influences through power of ideas, and also sometimes through money. EIGHT, being of the heart, influences through trust, as in banking. SEVEN, the number in which earth and water combine to form mud, reflects this peculiar factor by exercising influence negatively. SEVEN represents the influence of the masses, expressed in loyalty, and response to leadership.

Now the horizontal lines:

On top come the numbers of the head, 3, 6, 9. These are essentially independent, in three different ways. THREE is an individualist and a thinker who, without independence, finds it impossible to carry on. SIX, the man of commerce, is an organizer, and knows how to combine with others; in commerce he is frequently obliged to. But in the closest of combinations, his need for independence demands that he keep his own counsel. SIX is for this reason the number of shrewdness. NINE keeps his independence automatically; he usually thinks fast and has a grasp of situations (the head in relation to power); few can keep up with him.

The numbers of the middle line, 2, 5, 8, are again organizers. But being numbers of the heart, their gift for organization lies with people, rather than with material things. Here it will be observed how the central number, 5, in the vertical line of the organizer of *things* meets the horizontal line of the organizer of people, making FIVE the pre-eminent and balanced general organizer.

The bottom line, 1, 4, 7, numbers of the soil and stomach, is the line of reformers. These three are the numbers of manual labour, the people, the toilers. This is not a reference to any Victorian concept of 'the ignorant masses'; it is a simple analysis of an attitude of mind. Whether in literature (1), technical or manual labour (4), or agriculture (7), all on this bottom line know that their work can only be achieved by patient toil. This form of work being the most

6

common and necessary to man, these three numbers represent the people, and it is from them that reform springs. In ONE it expresses itself through ideas and in words. In FOUR it expresses itself in technical improvements to man's way of life. In SEVEN the influence of the masses—it expresses itself in the negative aspect of receptiveness to ideas of reform, and in research.

This gives the grid an additional set of dimensions. Thus:

	Individualists	Organizers (of things)	Influencers
Independents	3	6	9
Organizers (of people)	2	5	8
Reformers	1	4	7

Finally, the central vertical line (6, 5, 4) represents the body of man, the other two vertical lines the limbs. In that disease strikes the body rather than the limbs, SIX, FIVE and FOUR are those who need to take most care of their health.

As to the limbs THREE, TWO and ONE are likely to find that in the course of their lives they have needed the surgeon more than the doctor, and 2 is the number of surgery. These three numbers being the most sensitive (thought and air), they respond quickly to treatment, and are wise if they avoid taking medicine unless they really need it. NINE, EIGHT and SEVEN are likely to find they need the doctor more than the surgeon, and 8 is the number of medicine.

2

Nine Male Companions

The following descriptions of the character of each number are given in absolutes, i.e. each depicts what a person would be, if he had only one number. The descriptions are, of course, theoretical since such a situation can never arise.

Each person's character is a play of different numbers. A numerologist's skill lies in the ability to interpret correctly the interaction of different numbers in a person's character. For this it is necessary to understand the character of each number in its theoretical, absolute form.

Each description will be prefaced by the grid, marked with the lines with which each particular number has connections.

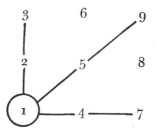

ONE (earth and air, stomach and thought) works best alone. He has patience (earth) in his work, but is quick-tempered (air) with others and dislikes interference or outside advice. Being rooted in the earth (line 1 to 7), with his mind reaching to the skies (lines to 3 and 9), he has practical ideas, knows what he wants to do and will not be deflected. He is self-contained. He seldom makes friends among his equals; he is not truly at ease unless people defer to him.

The three soil numbers (1, 4, 7) are moody, and ONE is irritable. Seeing himself as a being alone, he feels frustrated for no reason. He sees bad points before good. He has an impulse to set the world to rights, but is never satisfied. He is wiser with pen than tongue.

He has no sporting instinct, dislikes competition, and detests teams or committees, unless he is chairman. ONE *must* be Number One.

Connections are good: line to 9 (gift of utterance and money), line to 7 (the numbers of the people), and line to 3 (the arts and sciences). Having no access to 6 (commerce and law) or 8 (banking), ONE is a natural rebel against established thought and authority.

If required, he can command; and being without ambition in this respect (he is just as content to be left alone) his is the most attractive form of command, and the surest with men.

He is a good husband, provided he marries someone who defers to him. Absorbed in what he is doing, he is not fussy about domestic matters. He is an indifferent father, particularly to sons. In a ONE's house there is only room for one man.

ONE is the number of literature, whether as writer or reader, of invention, theory and new ideas. It is the number of the craftsman-artist. Sculpture, being manual labour, can also be present in ONE. It is the number of sole command.

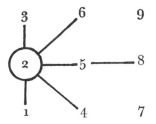

TWO (produce and air, heart and thought) is the number of duality, and contains a balance of the two sexes. This, in a man, means the presence of a feminine streak which, unless understood and controlled, can vent itself in petulance and vanity. TWO exercises strong powers of attraction and can be a strong personality. Many who are TWO, however, need consciously to cultivate manliness, lest they be distrusted by others. A manly TWO has a side of gentleness and grace, a love of fine things and quick, instinctive discernment. He is a person of emotion and imagination.

He sees both sides of a question, and being one of the three numbers which are organizers of people (2, 5, 8), this is an advantage, lying at the root of the attraction he exerts on others. He is sparkling and witty, and he likes to shine. Inwardly he sees himself as superior to others, and can become deeply depressed (line to 4, neurosis) if his self-esteem is wounded. He makes a distinction between acquaintances, of which he has many, and intimate friends, about whom, whether they are men or women, he can be possessive and jealous.

Being married to a TWO is not easy for a wife. TWO in a sense has an invisible wife inside him. Though he may be a passionate lover, he often feels no urge to marry. His best partner is someone domestically very thorough, because he is usually so himself. A marriage of convenience suits TWO best, so long as it is with a wife who does not strike attitudes.

TWO is not what the world would call a good husband, nor is he a good father, for though he may love his children, he pays attention to them only when it occurs to him.

He is artistic (line 3 to 1, the creative arts and sciences), and has an urge to externalize himself—thereby creating *two*. He is often a skilled amateur craftsman or mechanic. He is insistent on detail (connecting line to 4, detail, which is also a criminal line), often a perfectionist; and he is litigious (contact to 6, law, and 5, advocacy), sometimes to his disadvantage in the esteem of others. He needs to avoid speculation (absence of contact with 9). He is the most social of the numbers, more at home in town than in country (absence of contact with 7, agriculture).

TWO is the number of the mask, the professions connected with TWO being emblematic of duality. It is the number of diplomacy (the word means two-faced), the theatre (a mask and the real face), sculpture (an image of a man), architecture (a physical externalization of the mind), surgery (cutting things in two), espionage, and professional crime connected with duplicity. For a different reason (the human heart in air), it is the number of air navigation and of explorers.

Being the number of duplicity, TWO is at his best when wearing his mask, i.e. in action in his profession, wherein he assumes a rôle unlike that of ordinary life. Emblematically, a surgeon, when operating, wears an actual mask.

When TWO puts on his mask, the whole of him is concentrated on giving a superb performance, whether as a surgeon, an actor or an air pilot. When he takes his mask off and returns to private life, it will be found that this is either a muddle emotionally, or else so commonplace as to give no indication of the skill of which he is capable.

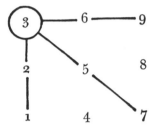

THREE (sunlight and air, head and thought) is a combination of TWO and ONE, containing elements of both in a well-adjusted balance. It is also the number of combination in general, or synthesis, in everything relating to creative thought. THREE is a person of many talents and wide interests (top horizontal line of the head). His mind is inclusive. He has energy, and seldom has to worry about health (sunlight and air). He prefers to leave details to others (absence of contact with 4, detail), and knowing how to devolve responsibility, he is a good administrator. His standards being high, he demands high standards of others, while not vindictive with those who let him down (no line to 4, neurosis).

Being the conjunction of air and sunlight, this is a number of happiness and ease. THREE is adventurous in thought and action (line to 6, risk, and 9, speculation), and can be incautious (absence of contact with 8, banking).

He is a natural leader, with power of appeal (line to 7,

the influence of the masses), but he is not a team man; he stands apart. His need to lead is compulsive and if deprived of leadership he becomes downcast and will take refuge in one of his talents.

He is a good husband and father. Though fastidious, his naturally happy temperament makes others around him happy. He likes a beautiful home. He is hospitable, and generous in his opinion of others but, though a lover of good company, he prefers it to come from professions other than his own (synthesis), and from cerebral people (line 3 to 9). Company apart, personal friends are not numerous, and they are seldom equals. The three numbers of thought (3, 2, 1) are similar in this respect.

Being married to THREE demands stamina, taste, and good management. It is hard work, but enjoyable.

In the numeral THREE, all the activities of TWO and ONE have a place and gather together. It is the number of the liberal arts and sciences, music (the composer rather than the executant), history and individual leadership. It is concerned with activities in which various arts combine, as in opera and ballet, and where varied branches of knowledge have to be brought into unity, as in the planning of new cities, and the writing of history.

Where the sciences figure in THREE, it is not so much in invention as in the sphere of demonstrative science: those who gather together what has been taking place in many fields of science, and demonstrate its practical application.

In the sense that he embraces so many of the finer things of life, combining this with talent and application as well as a love of good company, THREE is in some ways the most fulfilled of all the numerals.

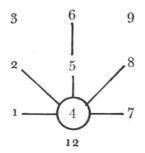

12

FOUR (earth and earth, stomach and activity) is the most fundamental of the numbers, the seat of accuracy, detail and technique. Here we have left the numbers of thought and ideas (3, 2, 1), and have entered a different sphere of human life.

FOUR is conservative and cannot abide generalizations (absence of line to 3, synthesis). He is a person of caution, only prepared to accept the proven, and it is with such matters that he deals. He is not cast down by adversity, nor does he give up easily. He is systematic, sometimes tiresomely so, over small things; he likes routine, above all in his home life. Being very much of the earth (at a conjunction), he is moody, and in extreme cases can become neurotic. FOUR is the number of neurosis.

This being the stomach number of the central vertical line of the human body, FOUR is fussy about his ailments, real or imagined, and very fussy about food. Not for nothing is FOUR the number of cooking; and he needs to marry a wife who can cook exactly what he wants.

He makes friends among his equals, among practical and stable people. His ideal wife is a cheerful person who brings light and colour into a home which would otherwise be drab, FOUR having little interest in beautifying his surroundings. He is a good husband, and a good though stern father—children *must* be systematic—and though he probably will not say so, he is intensely proud of his children when they do well.

On the grid he has no connecting line with THREE (individual leadership) or NINE (money and power). Though the most reliable of all on detail, he is not at ease when dealing with large worldly issues.

FOUR is the number of pure mathematics. He is also (vertical line) the most basic (earth-level) of the three numbers of earthy activity, who are organizers of material things (6, 5, 4). Thus, from his mathematics, come the laws of mechanics and, from this, machinery. Connected with everything to do with the soil, this is the number of physics and chemistry and, although not an original inventor himself, FOUR constantly improves on inventions in small but useful ways. Note that he has direct access to FIVE (organization and factories) and to SIX (commerce and law), both in need of FOUR's fundamentals.

In the central position at earth level, FOUR has a line leading straight upwards to the stars, and this is the number of astronomy. Being the master of detail concerned with the earth, FOUR is in addition the number of cartography and surveying.

Following from this, note the diagonals extending from FOUR. One leads directly to TWO (productive air), the number of air navigation, while the other leads to EIGHT (productive water), the number of marine navigation, both forms of navigation being alike dependent on FOUR's fundamentals—mathematics and maps.

On a more personal level, FOUR probably likes going to the theatre (2), provided he doesn't have to meet the actors and actresses; and while his cautious soul eschews speculation (no line to 9), he has direct contact with banking (8). Though seldom famous or wealthy, he is unlikely to be in want.

In a sense, FOUR is the number of science; yet as we saw earlier, demonstrative science—science expressed—lies with THREE. FOUR represents the fundamentals which lie at the root of the sciences, and in real life he is more likely to be the man behind the scenes, the draughtsman, surveyor, mechanic, accountant, those with a grasp of the minutiae which, unless correct, will bring larger matters to a standstill. In its most general sense, it is the number of detailed technical skill; and this can apply equally to a watchmaker, an accountant, a violinist, or (fine sense of taste) a chef. The number usually indicates someone in one of the professions or occupations concerned with mathematics or machinery. In addition, FOUR is an excellent teacher, being lucid and patient (earth).

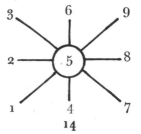

FIVE—produce and earth, heart and activity. And these four words are alone sufficient to show FIVE's strong points. He stands at the centre of things, both in the grid and in real life, at the intersection of the two lines of organization (of people and things). He is the principal organizer and co-ordinator.

He rubs shoulders easily with others, but has a tendency to be everybody's man, not in his own eyes, but in the eyes of others. Though adept at handling colleagues, and having many acquaintances, he does not feel a need for close intimacies, except in moments of adversity. He takes easily to being exposed to public gaze. He is conscious of the need to be fair to everyone, and this, when combined with his powers of organization, makes FIVE a particularly good leader or employer.

FIVE is the number of the military professions, industry and of anyone who is required to be skilled at large-scale organization, and show fairness in dealing with colleagues and employees.

As the central number, FIVE is the only one to have contact with all the others. It comes easily to him to control the rest, and is the number of politicians and statesmen. FIVE easily becomes a leader, though his leadership differs from that of THREE. FIVE's leadership is party or group leadership.

But while central in the grid, FIVE is the prisoner of the other digits. This is the number of subconscious frustration, providing the driving force which often shoots a FIVE into prominence.

Finally, if one thinks for a moment of the grid as a human face, it can be seen that FIVE, in the centre, represents the mouth. FIVE signifies the gift of utterance. In the case of a person whose work does not require utterance, this feature of FIVE as the mouth means the perfection of an ability which speaks for itself.

While SIX is the number of codified law and law-making, FIVE is the number of advocacy (utterance).

Whatever happens, FIVE is in the thick of it. If he uses utterance (a politician) rather than action (a general), he will irritate, and have detractors. In human life as a whole,

FIVE, a frustrated prisoner, is the irritant, fulfilling the same function as the grain of sand in an oyster.

.Having contact with all the numbers, FIVE likes to know a good deal about everything. He has an instinctive sense, however, which warns him not to go too deeply into any one subject. FOUR, the man of detail, regards FIVE as superficial.

When a FIVE boy is growing up, he is often not only flippant and irritating, but looks as though he is going to be a rolling stone that gathers no moss. He goes through phases (examining one number after the other), and seems incapable of sticking to anything, causing parental concern. When a FIVE boy is like this, it is important not to interfere with him, even though he may be scholastically backward. This is simply how FIVE grows up. By the time he is adult, he will have become an all-rounder. If he is over-interfered with as a youngster, especially by parents, he will suppress ambition into his subconscious frustration, and using his social gifts, will end as a *dilettante*.

Being married to a FIVE is to be married to a public figure. He is a reasonably good husband, but however much he may protest to the contrary, home considerations come last. Provided a woman doesn't mind this, well and good. The essential for FIVE is not to marry anyone jealous or possessive, or he will take emotional refuge in infidelity. He may have a streak of promiscuity as well, but he indulges it without much emotional involvement.

A typical FIVE is robust and energetic, a good sportsman, and he does everything he likes with zest. But it must be remembered that these central vertical numbers (6, 5, 4) represent the body, as opposed to the limbs, and have to be particularly careful about health. Where FOUR fusses about his health, FIVE usually doesn't; and with his multitude of commitments he is liable to overtax his heart (central number on the heart line), and have bouts of exhaustion.

SIX (sunlight and earth, head and activity) is the number of shrewdness and good judgment, commerce, enterprise and law. Standing at the head of the vertical line of organized earthly activity, his speciality is finance and commercial ideas (central cerebral number). Immediately below him on

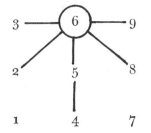

the vertical line stands industry (5), and SIX is the financier of industry. He is also the promoter of exploration and discovery (lines to 2 and 8, navigation). He is nearly always a congenial host and companion, but he is reserved, and on any matter of importance secretive, particularly in regard to money. He is a person capable of taking daring risks as an investor, promoter, or financier; and his judgment being good, he seldom makes mistakes.

The risks he takes, however, are such that he goes through mental torture (head number) waiting to know whether, metaphorically, his cargo has reached port. His entire life is risk, and being a controlled person outwardly, seldom giving release to his emotions (controlled by his head), he has to be careful to keep in a balanced state of physical health, or he is liable to be a victim of bodily disorders stemming from over-imposition on the nervous system. Many men who are SIX keep themselves physically stable by indulgence in rich food and wine.

It will be noticed that SIX, in his connections, is FOUR in reverse. Where FOUR starts on the grid from central fundamentals, and moves outwards and upwards as far as he can get, SIX starts from the central activity of the human mind in relation to the world he lives in (earthy activity), and moves outwards and downwards as far as he can get. He cannot reach intellectuals (1), and he is a fundamental mistruster of theory (1). Nor can he reach down to SEVEN, the negative influence of the masses. Nor, indeed, would he be wise to do so. If the masses were aware of the risks he took (often with their invested money), they would use their influence to incarcerate him.

Note on the grid how fundamental laws, having their basis in FOUR, rise to utterance (5, advocacy) and the exposition of the laws of mechanics in industry (5), thence upwards again to SIX, the central number of the mind, where laws are codified. There is a complement in SIX between instinctive judgment in respect of money, enterprise and discovery, and a sense of law, of which he is the codifier and upholder, a certain set standard of law and pratique being indispensable to the long-distance enterprises of which he is the promoter and financier.

On the left side, this complement is joined to another, connected with the arts and sciences (3), the theatre and architecture (2). While SIX is seldom a man of creative talent, he is a patron of the arts, a collector and a constructor; and he sometimes achieves fame (which he otherwise shuns) in this respect. Seldom able or willing to express himself in full, he leaves memorials to his unuttered thoughts in the form of collections and buildings. With his combination of risk and judgment, he is *avant-garde* in his tastes. In his home this produces a peculiar contradiction, in that as the upholder of law, he is by nature, in his manners and way of life, conservative and a conformist.

Though reserved and secretive, he is not selfish, nor is he a shifter. He is a connoisseur of food and wine, having direct links with fundamentals (4)—the cook.

As a boy, SIX may launch himself into study with single-mindedness (6, the central brain number). At no time is it more important than in boyhood for a SIX to be encouraged to develop his physique, which he may otherwise neglect.

SIX's best wife is a purposeful, strong-willed woman, with whom his private life is liable to be a tussle. She must not give in to him easily, either, or he may lose interest in her. He likes a (discreet) tussle. In his life, this kind of drama—otherwise lacking—acts as a tonic, taking his mind off the risks he is taking. The inner side of him, usually known only to his wife, is tender, and it is easy to hurt him. If for some reason his marriage breaks up, it can be the end of his career.

If he has the collecting instinct, his wife and children have to be resigned to being included as items in the collection. SIX *owns* things. He is a very good father, taking care of all his children's wants, and if they fail, he will regard it as his own failure.

SIX indicates enterprise in its widest sense, promotion and risk. It is the number of construction and commerce, codified law and law-making, and of legal judgment.

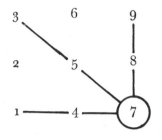

SEVEN (soil and water, stomach and power) is the number of agriculture—human power applied to the soil—and the character of SEVEN is that of a farmer. Like his brother-numbers of the soil (1, 4), he is patient and steady. He has a streak of laziness in him (soil and water—mud), and while he disciplines himself to regularity in his work, he dislikes it elsewhere. He is equable with others, despite moodiness. He enjoys friendships. If he has employees, he treats them as equals. He is a man of the people (line 1 to 7), and he sees himself thus.

Tolerant of others, he dislikes quarrels or argument. He has an absolute need for harmony in domestic personal relations, and in marrying needs to choose with this in mind.

Standing at the conjunction of earth and water, SEVEN has a negative aspect. He may be, and often is, a person of wide interests and learning, having contact with synthesis (3) in which, however, he is the spectator.

Being the number of agriculture, the most widespread and fundamental of all human occupations, SEVEN represents the influence of the masses, exerting power in the passive forms of loyalty, adhesion and response to leadership. Note in this respect how his line 7 to 3 runs through politics (5) to individual leaders (3), whom he prefers to politicians. This goes with his dislike of duplicity (no line to 2), men of sparkling wit (2), and people who take risks (no line to 6). Outwardly, SEVEN is severe.

He has a thorough grasp of money—line to banking (8) —and investment (9).

There is a streak of fatalism in SEVEN, pertaining to his character as a farmer. When a cyclone strikes, a farmer cannot, like a sea captain, receive an advance warning and take evasive action. If the cyclone strikes the farmer's fields, that is that. In the mentality of SEVEN there is an awareness that one may do one's best to reap a good harvest, but if the fates decree otherwise, there is no arguing about it. SEVEN is the number of introspection, whence research—consideration of the improbable yet conceivable.

A homely person, he is a good husband and father, and his children can be quite possessive about him. The negative aspect of his character inspires strong loyalties.

The farmer has to defend his fields, and SEVEN is the number of the defence of the nation, of gunnery, and of research connected with armaments and explosives.

All the numbers of defence, of which SEVEN is foremost, are in fact situated in immediate contact with each other in this lower right side of the grid: 4, technology, 5, munitions factories, 8, banking and shipping (supplies), and 7, gunnery and research.

In addition, SEVEN signifies work connected with forestry, soil and water conservation, the rearing of any kind of livestock, research in medicine, and in the products of the earth and ocean.

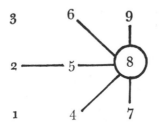

EIGHT (produce and water, heart and power) is the number of trust, implying trust over long distances (the human heart on water). Representing human power exercised through trust, it is the number of banking and insurance. Human power exerted on the organs of the body, symbolized by the heart, makes it the number of medicine and physicians.

Eight is the most reliable of the numbers. Regardless of what an EIGHT's occupation may be, he conveys to others an impression of reliability. He exerts power through good counsel, especially in money matters, and his steadiness (the heart on water, the ship) is reflected not only mentally but physically, since, unlike SIX, he does not take risks, and thus does not over-tax his nervous system. SIX and EIGHT complement each other, each possessing what the other lacks.

EIGHT is the number of marine navigation (produce on water), of seamanship, fleets, and navies. Movement at sea epitomizes EIGHT—steady, looking into the distance, and proceeding according to principles. EIGHT steers by principle (power) rather than law. If challenged, he can always ask a lawyer (direct access to 5 and 6) to defend him. This divergence is reflected daily in the life of EIGHT, particularly when he is a doctor. An influencer, he is one of those who causes laws to be changed.

Though a tower of strength where good counsel is concerned, never ask him for money. A person of the heart, he has a general interest in the activities of others, but distrusts intellectuals (no access to 1) and synthetic generalization (no access to 3).

As a banker, he is in touch with industry (5) and promoters (6), also with speculation (9), which he seldom indulges in. As a doctor, he communicates through the horizontal line of the heart with surgery (2) and has direct contact with the three numbers who stand most in need of his services—SIX, FIVE, and FOUR. As a member of the merchant marine, he is in touch with mechanical matters and maps (4), with defence in time of war (7), and with industry (5), whose products he transports.

He is abstemious in matters of food and drink. His home is his castle. The guardian of people's confidences, he is aware of the danger of too close an association with others in private life. For this reason, a child of an EIGHT can be lonely. Though generous to a fault, and the wisest of fathers, he does not care much for having his children's friends in and out of the house, and he mistrusts his wife's friends. He cannot stand muddle or unpunctuality.

Marriage to an EIGHT sometimes breaks down due to

what seems to be neglect on his part. At home he desires peace and quiet, and being in addition a disciplined person (principles), he can be a strain on others at home, almost a recluse. He needs a wife who in a tactful way takes the lead in his social life. In common with the other heart numbers (2, 5), he responds to social contacts in a way which is enlivening and health-giving, but being a number of water, socially he needs to be stirred to prevent stagnation.

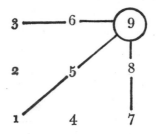

NINE (sunlight and water, head and power) is the number of power which is not intrinsically related to anything—sheer power. Unless applied or harnessed to something, it is simply heat (sunlight on water), or hot air. It is also the number of elimination; whatever one adds to it in numerology, NINE eliminates itself, leaving one with the number one first had. This means that NINE can achieve a great deal, or nothing.

From an early age he knows in an undefined way that he is a person who can put his hand to anything. Cases of him ending by achieving nothing are not frequent. Exactly what he will do, however, depends on his other numbers. Where he achieves nothing, he is apt to be a person of encyclopaedic knowledge (head and power), the enormity of which renders him incapable of putting it to productive use.

He is usually a mass of energy (sunlight on water, heat), physical and mental, and never even remotely worries about himself (no access to 4, plus the foregoing). He cannot stand men with a desire to shine (no access to 2).

When NINE is young, he is more of a problem to himself than others. Where parental control is concerned, the less the better. Every NINE has to find his way on his own, being very independent (top horizontal line). If he wants advice, he will ask for it. If he is repressed, or feels he is under paternal constraint (NINE knows how to get round his mother), he will prove rebellious to the point of doing everything he can to irritate his father and increase the latter's anxiety. He shares with FIVE the capacity to arouse deep parental concern.

NINE has this in him, though, that being unattached (9, power which is not attached to anything), and feeling a need for attachment, he is of a loving disposition. Once he reaches maturity a marked change of attitude occurs and he often becomes a loyal and devoted son.

NINE has a quality in his character which makes others suspect he considers them inferior. He unconsciously conveys an air of capability which in lesser men arouses jealousy. NINE being the number of money, he is in addition one of those people who seem to have money, even when they haven't, again prompting jealousy. Working in an organization, he needs to have trusted lieutenants, and wherever possible leave the talking to them. An aloof and powerful person, he is at his best in such a position. It is at the mid-levels that he arouses jealousy.

He makes a good but demanding husband, and needs to marry someone who can stand up to him mentally and physically, and will not mind his outbursts of irritation (heat). He forgives easily, and does not bear grudges (no line to 4), but in work, as at home, he is demanding of others, also punctilious. He is a loving but difficult father, and if he has a son who is a NINE, he is almost sure to make the same mistakes his father made with him. He also has to be particularly on his guard to constrain himself if he has a son who is a FIVE.

NINE is related to work concerned with power, such as atomic science, radiation and hydraulics; and with weights and strengths, as in engineering and large-scale construction. It is the number of investment and speculation, reliable and unreliable, being basically a number of all or nothing.

3

And Nine Females

For the sake of clarity, I have explained the numbers in terms of men only. The essential characteristics of each number apply to both sexes.

With women, however, there are some variants, more in some numbers than others. These variants now follow. They need to be regarded as *addenda* to the foregoing chapter, i.e. they are not complete in themselves, needing to be read in relation to the basic descriptions given in Chapter 2.

The soil numbers (1, 4, 7) are the numbers of masterful women. In each of these three numbers, this aspect takes a different form of expression.

ONE is a woman of reforming zeal, who sees what is wrong in the world around her, and is convinced she knows how to put it right. She believes she can command a place in public affairs, and in this she sometimes succeeds, though she is more wondered at than admired. Having a literary turn of mind, she is liable to be caustic. Outwardly she conveys an impression of hardness. She passes judgment with assurance of being right. She makes men feel small. Women respect and listen to her, though most are wary of associating with her.

Set upon a course, she pursues it relentlessly, to the exclusion of all else, but being a woman, is changeable. Suddenly, without warning, she will alter course, sometimes in the opposite direction; and peculiarly enough, she is still right. Useless to remind her that yesterday she was preaching the opposite of what she preaches today. Yesterday does not exist. She is, as ever, on course.

She is often artistic (line 1 to 3), very practical, and good with money (line 1 to 9). But she is dogmatic and, as she thinks, fundamental (line 1 to 7).

Her need to be Number One presents more difficulties than in a man. Due to her will to dominate people, she cannot keep friends; those closest to her are devotees. The only husband she can marry satisfactorily is a disciple, and even he will need patience. She is not interested in children.

If ONE is successful, meaning that she ends by having a suitable number of devotees, in later life she mellows, enjoying more contentment in age than in youth.

Where TWO as a man is a somewhat difficult number, due to the feminine streak in him, in a woman it is a number of great strength, due to the masculine streak in her— strength which may express itself physically, as in athletics or ballet dancing, or mentally, as in the power to convince. TWO is an organizer of people (central horizontal line), but her power of organization comes from the heart (central horizontal) and exists in the realm of thought and air (line 3, 2, 1). TWO being the number of discernment, this means that she is acutely perceptive of the motives and character of others, which is *how* she organizes. On occasions when she extends her organizational capacity beyond the home *milieu*, if rebuffed, she will withdraw, being extremely sensitive; and in any event, not being a cerebral number, she needs to confine such matters to women's affairs. This is the most emotional and sensitive of the women's numbers. It is a fine number for an actress, or indeed any woman in the performing arts, because it carries conviction, and she herself has an inward confidence (the masculine streak).

TWO sees life as herself and one other person, making *two*, whether it is a husband, a friend or a brother. Since she is quick on the uptake, intelligent and capable, it is essential she marry someone who commands her complete respect. If this breaks down, so will marriage.

If the man who dwells invisible in TWO is over-assertive, marriage becomes difficult. It is often replaced by a series of friendships, one after the other, in which TWO shows herself possessive, jealous and demanding. Since friendship or liaisons of this kind never last long, she is invariably the loser. (The same happens with men in whom the feminine streak of TWO becomes too assertive.)

There is something wayward about TWO. Not being moored to the earth, she is the kite which can cut loose. She is more interested in men than children, and is not always a successful mother.

Where the feminine side of TWO has too much headway, it can provoke religious ideas concerned with purity and celibacy. TWO having a passive quality in it, a predominance of femininity means passive combining with passive, which causes abnormalities.

One would expect excessive femininity to mean voluptuousness; instead, it means saintliness. When this happens, there is revulsion (covert or overt) against the husband, with serious effects on young children. Daughters can sometimes cope with this predicament, and of course, by following its direction, they can become nuns. For boys the effect is mentally emasculating, usually demanding intense struggle to break loose from mother-influence, provided they realize in time. As a woman, TWO's influence is very strong.

TWO *is* woman; the numeral represents the feminine gender. For this reason, feminine TWO is the most fascinating of all the numerals, and the most unpredictable. But whether feminine and saintly, or practical and somehow manly, she is a reminder that woman is a variant of man. As La Bruyère said: 'The most delightful intercourse a man can have is with a lovely woman who has the qualities of a gentleman.'

That is TWO. Because it is the most expressive among women's numbers, it tends to be the number of literature, if practised by a woman.

THREE dwells in the same atmosphere of happiness, ease and self-expression as her male counterpart, with plenty of hard work, which she enjoys. She is an admirable wife and mother, though when she has no career of her own she sometimes pines for one. Just as literature, where women are concerned, moved up from 1 to 2, so does surgery, when it is a woman surgeon, move up from 2 to 3.

The three cerebral numbers (3, 6, 9) represent the careers in which women compete successfully with men as equals, and can exercise authority over men without causing resentment. The women's professions which involve authority, such as hospital administration, are found bunched in 3, 6, and 9; and they are interchangeable. Women in authority need the cerebral numbers to a degree which men do not.

THREE shares the attributes of her male counterpart, save in the matter of being a leader. This aspect she confines to her home, or to her profession if she has one, i.e. by being good at it.

FOUR is one of the masterful women. Being the central number of the soil, her ideas about herself are fundamental and universal. If she sees the word 'mother' written down, she automatically reads it as 'motherhood'. When she is with child, she feels particularly elevated, superior to her husband. She loves routines, systems, cycles and seasons. There is method in everything she does, and from others in her home she demands compliance, to a degree no temperamental person can abide.

Since she often marries an easy-going man—her desire was to improve him, making him more methodical—and since she sometimes has temperamental children, she suffers torture from what she considers to be their vagaries; because she is fundamentally right—homes *should* be well run—she gains silent mastery over everyone about her.

She prefers daughters to sons. In fact, her general attitude to men is that they need improving.

Earlier it was observed how FIVE, albeit the central and commanding number, is also the numerals' prisoner. In a woman, the negative aspects of FIVE—frustration, and a capacity to irritate others—tend to be stronger than the positive attributes. FIVE feels a need to manage, organize and control; but as a woman her opportunities are limited. Not being a cerebral number, FIVE in a job is taken advantage of by men (also by women, if she is not careful), and she is never satisfied with what she is doing. She is liable to be a schemer. She is at her best when she has a great deal to do.

She is warm-hearted (central number on the horizontal heart line) and longs to help others, though when she does so, she nearly always does it the wrong way, producing complaint rather than thanks.

In recent years FIVE's problems have lessened slightly, with the opening of more careers for women. She can now become an advocate (5), or even a judge. Jobs are open to her in industry (5), and she can hardly fail to do well in the women's branches of the armed services (5). She is also in her element in anything to do with charities, social welfare, hygiene and research.

SIX and EIGHT to some extent change places with women. Where SIX in a man is the number of risk, in a woman it is the number of caution and steadiness. As was said before, SIX is the central brain number, and it is perfectly complementary, male and female. The mind of woman is caution; the mind of man is risk. Both are expressed in SIX.

Where trust, and the power of trust, finds its place in an EIGHT man, in a woman it occurs in SIX, the womanly number of banking, insurance, and medicine.

SIX, being cerebral, is a number of authority for women, who in this number excite no resentment when in authority over men. SIX (line 3 to 9, cerebral, line 6 to 4, organizing material things, diagonals to 2 and 8, navigation) is a born teacher, particularly as a woman. As a mother, SIX teaches her children well, and inspires much love and respect.

In a woman, SIX, rather than FIVE, tends to be the number of organization and management, being cerebral and without the frustrations of FIVE. SIX is good on committees and on anything involving groups. She can be successful in business.

SEVEN is another masterful woman, and this number is more difficult for her than for her male counterpart. Where the quality of introspection in a man leads to research, in a woman it leads to the evocation of waking dreams and ideals. SEVEN is the woman who dreams her child into the being she wills, and in the process drains the child of all drive or initiative. Where, in a man, the passive quality in SEVEN makes for harmony and a happy home, in a woman it becomes passive added to passive, which can produce distortions. It can in fact become a subtle form of aggression. SEVEN is the woman whose countenance does not alter when someone utters a swear-word, yet who inaudibly fills the room with her inexpressible distaste. This passive influence most commonly takes the guise of religiosity and self-pity, with a desire to refuse conjugal rights. Being a homely person, if religiosity sets in, SEVEN's home becomes not her castle, but her temple, making life unbearable for everyone else who lives in it. Her safest marriage is to a man in whose work she takes a keen personal interest, perhaps a professional man to whom she can be a secretary. In any case, a deliberate cultivation of outside interests is indicated, keeping dreams to the hours of sleep.

EIGHT and SIX to some extent reverse themselves in women. Thus EIGHT tends to be a woman's law and commerce number, and she takes calculated risks. But like her male counterpart, she is very reliable. She makes a good business woman, and if not helping her husband professionally, she often feels the need for a career of her own.

Her home is her castle, and the secret with an EIGHT wife is to ensure that one room in the house is entirely hers. She is liable to organize her husband and all those close to her, but since she will probably do this very well, resistance is pointless. She is a warm, generous-hearted mother, if somewhat over-protective—again, an organizer.

EIGHT has a very good balance between the feminine and the managerial, and if she has a career of her own, her *forte* is likely to lie in something with which women are concerned, such as women's journalism, *haute couture*, interior decoration, furnishing or gardens. Her best business partner is a woman who is a SIX, these two being complementary. EIGHT needs to avoid partnerships with emotional women (2), or with masterful women (1, 4, 7), who will be exasperated by her femininity.

NINE, in women as in men, means drive. She is a very

capable person, who may feel the need for a career. Even as a housewife and mother, however, she is the type of person who will treat that as a career. She is dependable, often a good sportswoman, and she understands her sons better than her daughters, with whom she becomes impatient if they are too feminine or changeable. Career women who need to exercise authority or impose discipline are at their best in NINE (cerebral), and she is particularly good at dealing with men, who like her. When dealing with women in an organization, she needs trusted lieutenants (like her male counterpart), and will be wise if she governs through them. She is a good motorist. She likes mechanisms (power, engines), and is often interested in science. Where money is concerned, she is either very good with it, or hopeless.

4

Finding the Lock

For many centuries—in fact, as far back into the past as numerology can be traced, which is to the beginning of written expression—attempts have been made to relate the subject to astrology, as by devising systems wherein each numeral is 'governed' by a planet. In some of the Buddhist countries in Asia, systems of this kind are still in use.

Actually, there is no tenable connection between the two. Astrology, allowing for its many imperfections, is based on planetary movement, on a system of movement which could be described as universal, and which is, for all we know, eternal. Numerology, on the other hand, is based on dates and names, which are mundane, local and temporary.

There is nothing universal or eternal about dates. Each religion has its own calendar; all of them are in operation in different parts of the world simultaneously; and all of them, in the eye of history, are temporary. Socrates did not give his date of birth according to the Christian calendar.

Each of us, however, is inseparably associated with certain numbers, and with certain sounds (names), which can be analysed by numbers. At the sound of our name, we turn, because it is *us*. Of all the days in the year, one is different from the rest, because it is *ours*, our birthday. It really *is* ours too. We are not expected to do much work that day, people give us presents, or we may throw a party. We associate ourselves with that day, with those numbers, and so do others who know us well.

Numerology is really a numerical analysis of how we see ourselves. When asked to state our date of birth, which of the world's various calendars do we use? Which numbers do we instantly *see* as being associated with us? When asked to state our name, how many of our given names do we state? How do we *see* ourselves, where our name is concerned? Do we think of ourself as Reginald Arthur Friedlander Pope? Or do we see ourself as Reginald Pope?

The commonest first question a numerologist is asked is, 'What name should I give?' The answer to the question is, 'How do you *see* yourself? By what name do you *think* of yourself?'

Because numerology is no more than an analysis of how we see ourselves in relation to numbers and sounds (names), it is of major importance to get this question answered satisfactorily.

With people who are not in the public eye—i.e. most people—this can be surprisingly difficult, especially in countries where it is the practice for children to receive many given names. There is also the difficulty that when asked, 'What name do you *think* of yourself as?' an amazingly high percentage of people have *never* thought.

Faced with this, there are various questions one can ask:

'How do you sign a cheque?'

'What name is on your passport?'

'If a police officer suddenly asks you to state your full name, how do you reply?'

'In a dream, if someone in authority calls you by name, what name does he use?'

This last, if the person is capable of answering it, is probably the best. The essential is to reach the person *as he sees himself*.

Numerology is of special value where parents are concerned, in that by working out the numbers of an infant, parents can be forewarned, long before a child can talk, what to be prepared for and what pitfalls to avoid. We noticed this earlier, in the particular caution which has to be exercised in respect of boys who are prominently NINE or FIVE.

When doing the numbers of an infant, if he has a string of names which it is unlikely he will use in adult life, it is necessary to ask the parents, 'Which name do you really *see* him as?'

It may be that, as he grows up, he will prefer another of

his names, or accidentally come to be called by one of these. In such a case, the numbers can be done again. At least the parents, in choosing *their* name for him, have been advised what to expect.

About names, there are various basic rules.

If Mr. Pope aforementioned signs his name R. A. Pope, use Reginald Arthur Pope.

If, like Bernard Shaw, a person signs himself G. Bernard Shaw, use George Bernard Shaw.

If a person has a very common name, like John Smith, and has a middle name which he never uses, include it, unless he has some rooted objection.

American men's names have acquired a formality unlike anything known in Europe. Most American men have three names, the middle one being represented in practice by an initial which is not dropped, however famous the person becomes—General George C. Marshall. In view of this formality, use *only* the initial of the middle name, unless the person particularly asks for the whole of it to be included. Since he may often do this out of respect for his father, and not because he feels it actually represents *him*, take the precaution of doing both—George C. Marshall, and George Catlett Marshall, and you will quickly see which one is right.

Occasionally, a man is known throughout his life by his surname only. Gandhi is a case in point. After childhood, no one used his personal name. With such persons, use the surname and the *initials only*—M. K. Gandhi—taking the initials he uses when signing his name.

Where a man is known by his initials, as with Lord Birkenhead, universally known as F.E., spell out the words in full.

However much anyone is known by a nickname, do not use it. Work from his registered, or baptismal name, and find out how he *sees* himself in regard to it.

Do not use diminutives, unless they are registered as such. If a man is registered as Rob, use it; but if he is universally known as Robbie and registered as Robert, use Robert.

Do not use titles unless, as sometimes happens in France and Italy, the title is also the surname. It is the personal name and the surname which count. Thus, if doing Jean,

Duc de Montesquieu, use Jean Montesquieu, unless he uses the 'de' in his signature, in which case include it. If the title is that of a town or province, and the man signs nothing else (as with an English peer), use the personal name and the surname.

Throughout the world, a majority of women change their names on marriage. Either they take their husband's surname and drop their own, or, as in Spain, Portugal, Latin America and the Philippines, they may add their husband's surname to their own. In either case, their name number changes.

When doing the numbers of an unmarried girl, begin with her personal name *only*—how she is called, how she *sees* herself and is seen—and lay it out on the grid in the manner which will be explained in Part II, Chapter 1. This is the name she is most likely to carry through her life.

Then, do another grid, with her personal name and her maiden name together. By comparing the two grids you will have a fairly clear idea whether or not she will have a career of her own, especially after taking into account her date of birth and her balancer (this word will be explained in the next chapter).

If she looks like having a career, there is the possibility she will, for professional reasons, keep her maiden name, in which case this can be analysed. If a career seems unlikely, there is nothing much numerology can do with any degree of certainty until she marries, when she can be studied with her personal name and her husband's surname, with her maiden name retained or removed as the case may be.

Where, as in Iberian tradition, the maiden name is retained on marriage, if the word 'and' is included (*y* or *e*) it may be ignored, unless in the case of a woman who, in public affairs or as a director of a company, deliberately uses it and is publicly known with it.

In the case of an Overseas Chinese girl who uses Roman letters to write her name, if she formally uses her husband's surname in front of her own, include it. Otherwise, it is better to work on her three-character name prior to marriage.

5

Inserting the Key

Each of us has three principal numbers: the date of birth, the name, and the sum of these two, which is the balancer.

The birth number indicates a person's directional sense, the type of driving force within, the mentality with which he looks at things, and the aptitudes which come naturally, with little need for conscious development.

The name number is the personality. It is the person as he knows himself to be, and as he is seen by others, the effect he has on others. It is the most significant of the three numbers. The theoretical descriptions of the nine numerals given in Chapters 2 and 3 come closest to actuality when they are name numbers.

The balancer represents an aspect of a person's character liable to be of importance in work. It sometimes indicates the career; more often it indicates an aspect of a career which can be of crucial importance. In some people, it surfaces as a hobby or talent.

The clearest analogy of the three numbers is to imagine them in relation to one of those small, swift-moving, one-man sailing vessels used in Polynesia, in which man and vessel (name, personality) are one. Aft he has a small steering oar (number of birth, direction), and to one side a single outrigger (balancer) giving stability.

Whatever the language, use whatever happens to be the alphabet, applying numbers to letters in their sequential order. Where the Western European languages are concerned, use the full Roman alphabet of 26 letters, even when doing names in languages such as Italian, Spanish, and Portuguese, which officially omit certain letters. In these languages, persons of Germanic, Hungarian, or English ancestry have names which include the missing letters, thus these are effectively in use—as in telephone directories, for instance.

In Asia, use the full Roman alphabet for Overseas Chinese and others who normally sign their name in English, French or Dutch spelling and who *think* of their name in Roman script.

When faced with an array of numbers, as in numbers applied to a person's name, add them and continue doing so until they are reduced to one digit.

Similarly with a date. Express it numerically, then reduce it to one digit by addition, viz. 13th December 1939, equals 13121939 which, by addition, equals 29 which becomes 2 + 9, 11 and then 1 + 1 which equals 2.

Here is a table of the Roman alphabet in relation to numbers:

1	2	3	4	5	6	7	8	9
A	B	C	D	E	F	G	H	I
J	K	L	M	N	O	P	Q	R
S	T	U	V	W	X	Y	Z	

II

THE DOOR OPENS

I

To have a Mind

As a basis for demonstration, I propose to summon up a great man of the past, Francis Bacon, the father of experimental philosophy.

The choice is emblematic. Though his writings and thought influenced the whole domain of natural science and he ushered in the scientific age in which we live today, he was also, strange to relate, keenly interested in the meaning of numbers.

He was born on 22 January 1561. In setting out a date, it is advisable to break it into its component parts, since these indicate how the final digit is arrived at, and can reveal clues. Thus:

22 January 1561

4   1   4

9

9 is the number of power—sheer power, which if not attached or harnessed to something is virtually useless, rather similar to unmined gold. When 9 occurs as the birth number, it signifies a person capable of putting their hand to almost anything and doing it well, in that in this position 9 brings power and strength to what a person undertakes. The question is: will the person do anything at all?

In this case, it looks as if he will, this 9 being made up of two 4s, indicating a grasp of fundamentals and perhaps science, joined by 1, the number of literature and invention. This is a 9 by birth who, with any luck, is going to achieve something.

In order to find out in what field, we next turn to the name:

FRANCIS BACON
6 9 1 5 3 9 1   2 1 3 6 5
(34)   (17)
7   8
6

By name he is 6, the number of law and commerce. To obtain the balancer, we add:

Birth:	9
Name:	6
15	Balancer: 6

Note how 9 eliminates itself.

Observe too how, when 9 is the birth number, it automatically means that the number of name and balancer are the same, indicating a person who identifies himself completely with his work, and who is liable to be similarly identified by others. This situation, of producing people who give themselves completely to what they do, is the principal way in which 9, the number of power, exerts itself through them.

Here is a person whose work and personality will probably be concerned with either commerce or the law (6), and who will bring power (9) to bear on what he does. The fact that he rose to be Lord Chancellor of England, head of the legal profession of his country, is a somewhat startling outcome, which could hardly happen to everyone with such numbers. But it shows in a reasonably emphatic manner how the numbers work. The reader familiar with Bacon's life will also remember his active financial interest in promoting (6) the first plantations in America, and the Hudson's Bay Company.

This, then, is an example of the bare bones of a person's numbers:

22 January 1561	Direction	9
Francis Bacon	Personality	6
Sum	Balancer	6

Now, we examine the details of the subject's personality, as expressed in the name.

This is done by placing the name on the grid, letter by letter, setting a ring round each letter's appropriate number. This done, one notes the row of numbers bearing the greatest number of rings, and draws across it the stress line.

Some names have more than one stress line, in that two or more rows have an equal number of rings. Where this occurs, all lines of the same maximum strength need to be placed on the grid. Each stress line has a special meaning.

With the name of Francis Bacon, the outcome is this:

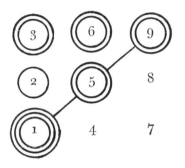

This stress line, from 1 (ideas), through 5 (gift of utterance), to 9 (power and money), is the commonest line of worldly success.

Really, the stress lines should be thought of as arrows, with tip and tail, the tail being weighted, i.e. the end number with the heavier amount of rings.

This stress line, weighted in 1, signifies a person who from humble beginnings can rise to power, money or fame, all or severally. This applies to a person who has to struggle up.

In the case of Francis Bacon, who as second son of the Lord Keeper to Queen Elizabeth I was born to some affluence, the stress line in this (arrow) direction is more likely to mean the successful projection of new ideas. This, if one thinks of it, means making something out of nothing, and is similar to rising from humble beginnings to power.

These ideas will be well-formed (5), delivered in a manner

others can understand (5), and he will never want for money (9).

Note the perfect balance of the head numbers (3, 6, 9), each with two rings round it.

Perfect balances of this kind are extremely significant in numerology. This one means the equable, the acceptable and the widespread. Being a double-ringed balance means a mind of tremendous power and wisdom. Here is a person whose thought is going to possess extraordinary balance and capacity. It is almost certainly going to be universal, though being entirely along the line of the head (top horizontal), with scant relation to the daily affairs of men (absence of 4 and 7), it is liable to be thought which, though widely accepted, will not be especially understandable except to the educated.

Next, note the strong numbers of the creative arts (3, 2, 1), with the accent on literature (1). That strong 1, on the stress line, is precluded from being an inventor or a sculptor (manual labourer) by having the three perfectly balanced head numbers (3, 6, 9, each with two rings round it). This is very much a man of the world, familiar with the arts and sciences (3), a lover of fine things (6), with very wide knowledge (9, encyclopaedic, in perfect balance of head numbers). This makes for too general a personality to be an inventor, who is more concentrated on particulars.

The more one looks at this grid, the more it suggests new ideas of great breadth expressed in the form of literature.

Now, hovering in the wings are his other two basic numbers: the number of birth (9), and the balancer (6). Though these numbers are *not* included in the grid, they are having an influence on it. In this case they are accentuating his already strong 6 and 9, indicating a life in public affairs concerned with the law and commerce (6) and power (9).

At first it suggests a very literary and artistic lawyer (all the arts numbers, 3, 2, 1, represented). But the stress line is weighted in 1, meaning this is the wrong way round. This is going to be a writer (1) on a wide range of subjects (3, 6, 9), who expresses himself with the exactitude of a lawyer (6). This points plainly to philosophy.

But he will also express himself with great artistry (2 and

3), in a vivid and colourful way. Here is the mind of a philosopher whose self-expression will scintillate, for all its legalistic exactitude; and indeed no philosopher has ever expressed himself so accurately in words of such magic.

Having all three arts numbers, he is almost certain to be keen on the theatre (2); and we find that one of his favourite diversions was organizing pageants and revels.

Though a lawyer (6 by name and balancer) and a man of power (9 by birth), he will be more interested in things of the mind (3, 6, 9 in perfect balance, in doubles) than in wielding power in public affairs (absence of 8 and 7, both of them numbers of power and influence). Absence of 8 and 7, in a set of numbers as powerful as this, means either, one who eschews the wielding of political power, or is defective in the manner in which he does so.

The power of Bacon's mind was so tremendous * (perfect balance on the cerebral line in doubles is almost unbearably strong) that in public affairs many distrusted him, feeling he was on a plane above them, while in making a speech in Parliament, he could never spare a jest (arts numbers), and this often deflected men's minds from the wisdom of what he was actually saying.

Men with perfect balance in the cerebral numbers in doubles—it is uncommon, and remembering that, in addition, he has two more 6s by name and balancer, and another 9 by birth, it is almost overwhelming—trip up on quite small and simple matters, which a less clever man would know about, and be prepared for. This is the type of person who constructs a trans-continental highway, yet when going for a walk, trips over in a pothole.

His weak point is probably going to be impatience with technical detail (absence of 4), and here it will be remembered that his birth number (9) was made up thus: 4—1—4. This is a slight compensation, indicating that he is going to apply himself to technical detail, though it will probably be onerous.

* When Bacon was in his 'teens, Nicholas Hilliard, the 'master limner of the age', painted his miniature, and was able to converse with the boy at some length. When he finished the miniature, Hilliard wrote round the rim: 'Could one but portray his mind!'—*Si tabula diretur animum mallem.*

Of note, too, is the fact that 4 is the number of astronomy, the field in which he made his one serious error. In middle life he reversed his earlier judgment that the earth revolved round the sun.

For a person of his nature, occupied with the natural sciences and the laws (6) governing them, absence of 4 is a disadvantage, his heel of Achilles, as in public life his inattention to detail in regard to moneys received, and gifts made to him in office, precipitated his downfall as Lord Chancellor.

Absence of 7, on the other hand, in a person with such strong and balanced numbers, usually turns out to be an advantage. It means a tireless person (7 is the number of laziness), in his case accentuated by having a healthy body (6 with a calm mind).

It will be complained that all this is hindsight. It is. But in numerology it is from hindsight that one develops foresight, particularly from the study of people of the past, whose achievements and character are known, enabling one by careful examination to observe how the numbers operate.

2

Drawing Distinctions

Each stress line has variant meanings, dependent on the balance between the three numbers on it.

Here are the variant meanings of the stress line 1 to 9.

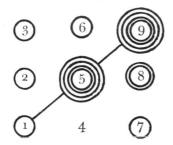

In this, the weight is in 9 (arrow diagonally downward). This indicates a person usually born in favourable circumstances (9, power and money), capable of putting across ideas which he may not have invented, and which may not necessarily be new, but who does so with effect and concentration. He is a person prepared to make material sacrifices for what he believes in, and is inclined to do so in disregard of his wife and family.

Equally, from a sound background (9), he is a person prepared to knuckle under to adverse conditions, and will expect his family to do likewise.*

The above is the grid of Sir Christopher Wren, architect of St. Paul's Cathedral, London. Note the massy weight of 9 (power) and strength of expression (5), also the perfect balance on 3, 2, and 1, indicating great mastery in the arts

* The President of the United States, Richard M. Nixon, has this line, and the members of his family have experienced precisely its effects.

and sciences. This stress line, weighted in 9, indicates integrity and an absolute need to make up one's mind without interference.

With everyone on this line, whether weighted upward or downward, a guiding urge is the exposition of truth. Whereas, weighted in 1, it leads from the particular to the general, when weighted in 9, it leads from the general to the particular.

In Wren's case, it was extreme concentration on projection of style, to a degree at which, by looking up at a ceiling, one could see from its proportions that only one man in the world could have designed it.

And this was achieved despite having to knuckle under throughout his life to the inferior opinions of men who did not share his vision. St. Paul's is Wren's splendid monument, but had he been allowed to build it in his own way —the plans, known as the Great Model, are extant—it would have ranked as one of the most perfect structures on earth.

His absence of 4 means impatience with detail, and in this position as the only missing number it usually implies good health. An intriguing aspect of it here is that Wren gave up astronomy (4) in favour of architecture.

Further to explain this concentration on the particular, let me do another one. Here is the grid of the great Belgian writer Maurice Maeterlinck:

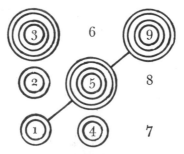

Here is a truly marvellous mind—powerful 3 and 9 in balance (four rings round each) on the head line (3, 6, 9)— utterly unconcerned with financial matters (absence of 6, commerce, and 8, banking), with great artistry (strong 3, 2, and 1), power of expression (5), and command of detail (4).

This mind is concentrated on the particular (line 9 to 1 downwards), and on truth. The outcome was *The Life of the Bee*, with its terrible exposition of the philosophy of beauty and horror—a work of art (3, 2, 1) and technical knowledge (4).

A great human mind concentrated on a bee—this is the quintessential meaning of this stress line when it occurs downward with a clothed 5.

Here is the same line equally balanced at both ends, with 5 stronger in the middle:

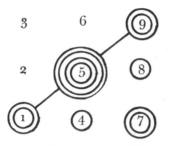

This means a person given to searching self-examination, and who is frequently troubled by conscience, being somehow unsure of himself, though having no real reason to be, this being a line of worldly success. He cannot help himself, however; he worries about his motives.

The foregoing is a particularly good example of how this very feature can be used to good purpose, being the grid of the novelist Graham Greene, who made conscience the theme of much of his finest work, in particular his masterpiece, *The Power and the Glory*.

Next, here is the line in perfect balance:

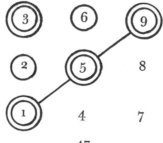

Where perfect balance occurs on these numbers when they are *not* on a stress line, it means exceptional ability to handle money, whether one's own or public funds, skill with propaganda and fund-raising.

Where the same occurs *on* a stress line, as above, it means a person who seems to go through no period of immaturity, who as a young man carries authority beyond his years, and whose work is as finished and mellow when he is young as when he is old. The grid in question is that of my father, the composer Eric Coates, of whom the foregoing was true.*

Perfect balance has exactly the same meaning when it occurs on this stress line:

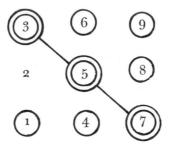

This is the grid of the great English actor Sir John Gielgud. No one ever remembers seeing an immature Gielgud performance. These are people who somehow escape immaturity, at least in the eyes of others.

Then there is this one:

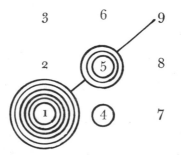

* Were one to take my father's first song success, *Stonecracker John* (1909), and the full score of his march for the movie *The Dambusters* (1955), one could put the latter's date on the former, and no one, from the inner content, would notice the mistake. The voice, speaking in music, was completely consistent.

Note that 9, with the line like this, is naked. This means a successful person for whom money (9) is unimportant, who does not have to worry about money, and may not even have to handle it—it may be handled by his wife, or someone else. He has no interest whatever in wielding worldly power (9).

In this particular case, of course, it is a person with new ideas (1) on an enormous and challenging scale (so many rings round it), with a compelling gift of expression (5), though so absorbed in what he is doing as to be virtually oblivious of everything else (so many naked numbers in relation to multi-ringed 1, a giant intellect).

The only clue to what he is concerned with is that small 4, the only other clothed number, representing pure mathematics and astronomy; and the grid is that of Sir James Jeans, the astronomer who explained the universe in terms of mathematics, in his *The Mysterious Universe* with his wonderful gift of conveying (5) vast ideas in simple language.

Lastly, there is this variant:

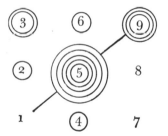

This is the stress line of melancholy amid success, of never-satisfied striving, and of a self-induced sense of frustration. Such people are seldom in real want (especially with such gift of utterance as is shown in that strong 5), yet they do not convey happiness to those around them.

Whenever this stress line is weighted in 9, it indicates a capacity to make material sacrifices for what one believes in; and where 1 is naked, as in this case, the tendency is intense. Because this downward arrow on stress line heads to 1 (self), but does not reach it—1 is naked—there is something unreasoning in its urge to sacrifice. The course taken nearly always leads to financial reward in the end (whichever way it points, this is a success line), but it can involve distress to self and others.

Since this is a person still living, I leave this one anonymous. As the grid reveals, it is someone highly gifted and intelligent. Many other examples of the peculiar tendency of this downward line could be cited.

Where women are concerned, these stress line variants have the same meanings, except that they tend to apply 'within the walls' and not, as in a man, to external matters. Thus, the immediately preceding variant, in a woman, means a person who is liable to disapprove of her husband's code of conduct and seek to impose her own will on his— often without success. It is a line of disruptive marriage, unless handled with great self-control.

Stress line 1 to 9, weighted either way, is not an easy line for a woman in marriage. Its meaning when weighted in 1 will be explained in Chapter 8.

Before leaving this stress line, a word must be said about 5, the number in the middle. Depending on the number of rings around it, 5 merely adds strength to the line. Where 5 has no rings round it, yet the stress line runs through it between 1 and 9, it denotes a person who will try to achieve the objects of 1 to 9 or 9 to 1, but will fail, either due to inability to convey his ideas (5, utterance), or due to insufficient mastery of subject (5).

Perfect balance on 3, 2, 1, which we observed in Wren, can also mean exceptional social gifts, or entrepreneurial ability. However it occurs, it is extrovert.

3
Among the Foremost

The aim in these chapters is to demonstrate how to read grids. This being so, I shall in some instances leave out birth and balancer and will also sometimes hold in reserve the name of the person being examined. This is done purposely, to enable the reader to think in relation to the grid.

Here is a man, and he is by name a 7:

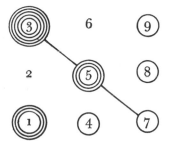

The almost unwieldy weight of 3 (arts and sciences, history, individual leadership) connecting on a downward-sloping arrow through 5 (gift of utterance) to 7 (the passive influence of the masses) shows immediately that this is an individual leader, above or separate from party politics, capable of commanding loyalty and a public following. The perfect balance of his numbers of influence and power (9, 8, 7, each with one ring round it), shows a person capable or desirous of wielding great general influence, enabling one to say that the response of the masses (7) to him will be more than considerable. Capable of commanding mass appeal, he will almost certainly be an important national leader.

The absence of 6 (love of fine things), combined with absence of 2 (the theatre and gentleness) suggest a stern character, incapable of duplicity or manoeuvring (absence of 2). The same absence of 6 and 2 indicates that his powerful 3 will be connected more with the sciences than the arts, and (3 in relation to 1) history. He will probably have literary talent (strong 1) in connection with history (3), though literature will not figure as his main occupation (1 is not on the stress line).

He is not an equable character to deal with (absence of 6 in the head numbers, and a disproportionately large 3—the head numbers need to be more balanced for equableness).

Not only commanding a mass following, but having in addition a wide knowledge and understanding of his people (1, 4, 7, the numbers of the people, all represented), he is liable to be impatient of anyone standing between him and the people (note the tremendous downward force of the arrow, with 5 not specially strong), in particular—one would suspect—of politicians and functionaries (5). He is liable to be authoritarian.

In his private life he will never have to worry about money (strong line from 1 to 9, and with 8—banking—represented). Though he is a capable organizer (5 and 4 on the vertical line), with a grasp of detail (4), he is not good at the money aspects of organization (absence of 6), and being an authoritarian he is the type of leader who will say, 'No money? Find some!'

His name being a 7 strengthens his 7 on the grid, and this last having all the numbers around it represented means an interest in defence, research, industry and agriculture, all or severally. This is a mind with a very complete grasp of a country's needs.

As an organizer of people (horizontal central line) he is a man's man (absence of 2, with 8 present), more suited to military than civil organization, and probably without much personal appeal to women. In fact, this, coupled with his rather stern nature (absence of 6 and 2) suggests that in addition to being a national leader he will also be a military man.

Having come so far, let us now bring in his two other

basic numbers. By birth (22 November 1890) he is a 6, which with that grid means definitely not commerce, but a bent for law and (the authoritarian) order. All told, a somewhat formidable figure. 7, his personality, is a number which commands respect and loyalty. Outwardly severe, yet his children are likely to be proud and fond of him.

His balancer (6 + 7) is 4, which with that grid comes down absolutely on (in relation to strong 7, research) the details of military technology, which is liable to play a vital part in his career.

This is Charles de Gaulle, and it will be remembered that he first rose to prominence as an expert on armoured tanks, the key factor which led on to his ultimately becoming the ruler of France, and the deviser of a new constitution (birth number 6, the codifier of law).

This, incidentally, is a good instance of how the balancer often represents an aspect of a person's career which may prove of determining importance.

Next, his great counterpart on the other side of the Channel.

He signed his name Winston S. Churchill, meaning, for numerological purposes, Winston Spencer Churchill. Here he is:

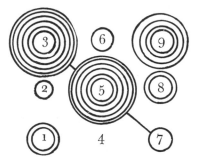

Bear in mind, first of all, that this is a longer name than that of Charles de Gaulle. The rings around the numbers in a person's name have to be seen relative to one another. This, in a person with a short name, means that each ring bears more weight than in a long name like this. In other words, never compare the weight of the numerical rings in one person's name with the weight of those in another; it means nothing. The grid presents something which is personal and internal, and must be considered solely in terms of itself.

In Churchill one sees the same stress line as in de Gaulle: from the born leader (3), through gift of utterance (5), to the passive influence of the masses (7), indicating a leader of great popular appeal. It will be noticed, however, that where de Gaulle's powerful 3 was two rings stronger than his 5, and he had an absence of 6 and 2, indicating a stern leader, Churchill's 3 and 5 are balanced (six rings round each). In a national leader—and this stress line is nearly always that of a person of appeal, whether national, regional, or in a village—such a balance between 3 and 5 shows a born leader who is able to conduct affairs *through* politics and politicians. Though really too large for politics, he can play the party man if need be.

He has a soft spot (2) and a love of fine things (6), besides having all three numbers of the arts (3, 2, 1), indicating—in his 3—a culturally mellow and fully expressed person. Having in addition all the numbers of an organizer of people (2, 5, 8), though a born leader and man of power (9), he has kindliness and heart (horizontal central line).

All men with this stress line on a downward arrow, however, are difficult to deal with face to face. There is something about them that is a little larger than life. To say they do not suffer fools gladly is an understatement. Only those who are alert and sure of their facts can get on with them, and then only as supporters, not equals.

Note Churchill's 1, which with 2 and 3 both represented, and with 2 (the social number) tranquil, will certainly mean literature; and this being the grid of a political leader, his literary bent will be reflected most strongly in history (3). He will also be a generous writer—3, generous in opinion of others, and strong 9, the warm-hearted—as evidenced in his finest historical work, *Marlborough*.

Note that his numbers of power (9, 8, 7), though strong, and reinforced by two extra 7s, one from his birth (30 November 1874), the other as his balancer, are not evenly balanced. This means that, unlike de Gaulle, whose influence was general, Churchill's influence on his people is specific in relation to time and circumstances—in his case, times of war. This is not the kind of perfectly balanced influence which inaugurated the Fifth Republic and devised a new constitution.

Observe now Churchill's absence of 4, and how this absence is not compensated for, either by birth or balancer. This means impatience with detail. Being uncompensated for has the effect of strengthening it. This is a person who cannot abide being held up by quibbles over detail, and who is inclined to regard masters of minutiae (4) as obscurantists. This, in any event, is the meaning when seen in relation to a name of strong numbers. In a person with less pronouncedly strong numbers, it means simply inattention to detail. People with such a total lack of 4 as this are usually aware of their shortcomings on detail, and sometimes decide to get down to it. The outcome is liable to be comic. This was true of Churchill.

Churchill by name was a 9, and he is a perfect example of one. His 9 is reinforced by a strong 9 on the grid, plus a strong 5, both these numbers having the same problems in youth. More attached to his mother than to his father— the typical youth of 9 and 5—he reached maturity to become a loyal and devoted son. Not really interested in school, he grew up to seem (in other people's eyes) brilliant but unreliable, reaching young manhood as one of those infuriatingly (5, the irritant) brilliant men who will probably achieve nothing. He then proceeded to confound his critics by turning into a true 9, the person who can put his hand to almost anything and do it well. The war leader, the orator, the statesman, the historian, the artist and the bricklayer—first-rate in each.

His two extra 7s (birth and balancer), when offset against the grid of someone who is clearly going to be a national leader, will almost certainly refer to defence, though not, in this case, to the technical details of it (absence of 4), so much as in a general grasp of large issues concerned with it, with reference to the armed forces in general (5), and probably with special reference to the navy (two rings round 8, marine navigation, close to a strong 7).

To suggest that this stress line in two national leaders is

not entirely chance, here briefly are two more. First, France's best-loved leader of this century, Georges Clémenceau:

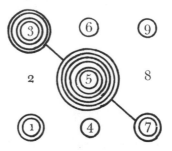

Herein one sees the born leader who can work *through* politics, though really a person who is above politics.

Note the balanced absence of 2 and 8. This in a man of great public appeal (stress line 3 to 7) indicates a person who, though admired and a leader, is not a successful organizer of people in daily life. It means impatience with the day-to-day disputation and wrangling of men. Not for nothing was he called 'the Tiger'. It also represents the statesman, as opposed to the politician. Men with this feature in their grid do not plead; they state.

A person of wide views (all three head numbers) and fiercely independent (horizontal line of independence, fully clothed, with absence of 2 and 8), he had all the numbers of the people (1, 4, 7); and though politically erratic, with ups and downs (absence of 2 and 8, unsuited to dispute), he commanded a following because he was always understandable (that tremendous 5). I shall return to the Tiger later.

Finally, a contemporary from Asia, the distinguished and successful Prime Minister of Singapore, Lee Kuan Yew:

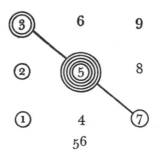

Once again, the born leader capable of commanding a following—stress line from 3 (the leader) through gift of utterance (5) to the response of the people (7). His 5 being much stronger than his 3, he is, though really above politics, eminently capable of working through a political party, somewhat following the Taoist principle that 'the greatest leader of men is always *behind* them'. In keeping with this is the fact that he owes his position to the party which he himself largely created.

He has only one head number (3), indicating a leader who pursues specific aims, on which he concentrates to the exclusion of other matters. As a leader, the direction of these aims is liable to lie in the field of culture in its widest sense (3, 2, 1, the numbers of the arts, all represented). Being in control of a multi-racial republic with four major languages (English, Chinese, Malay and Tamil), his first task must obviously lie with social, educational and cultural problems; and it is here that he has achieved his most notable success to date, in giving Singapore a sense of social cohesion which it never had as a British colony.

His period of rule in Singapore will also always be remembered in connection with housing for the underprivileged —one of the world's largest and most successful public housing schemes—housing (2 and 3) being integral to culture.

Though interested in the development of industry (5) and the armed forces (5), this is secondary to his main aims, which are cultural. His weak points are banking and the port (absence of 8), financial policy (absence of 9 in relation to 1), economics and commerce (absence of 6), and the details (absence of 4) of industry and commerce. On these matters he must take advice from others, which he has the capacity to do (3 in relation to a much stronger 5 on the stress line).

Though by profession an advocate (5), he is not a codifier of law, or maker of new constitutions (absence of 6). He took the laws as he found them, and happily they were in good order.

He is very much a civilian ruler (2 and 5 on the line of the organizer of people, with 8 missing). In a leader, as was seen with de Gaulle, 5 and 8 with absence of 2 suggests rule of a military character (the man's man). The other way round, it means someone who is pronouncedly a civilian. Lee Kuan Yew, so far as I know, has never worn a uniform.

Like Clémenceau, he is by name a 5, the number of politics, organization and advocacy.

By birth (16 September 1923) he is 4, in his case a technical perfectionist, domestically very organized. His balancer is 9, which in a person who is not a scientist, and in relation to a strong 5, suggests ability to wield power.

It will be noted that each of the four men selected to demonstrate the meaning of the stress line from 3 to 7, with weight on 3, has one particular feature in common. Each in his own time and place stands unique, seen by others as head and shoulders above the ordinary, each rather formidable as an individual. This is the most powerful of all lines of public leadership and usually the most beneficent, in that 3, where the line is weighted, is the number of happiness; and 3 in power feels spiritually at ease, immediately creating confidence among those around him.

These principles apply in their context. Here we have dealt with national leaders. The principles apply equally in regional and provincial spheres. Men with this line seldom worry about money. Having confidence in themselves and others, they feel money will look after itself.

When the stress line 3 to 7 is weighted in 3, but with 5 naked, it designates a person striving to attain public acclaim or a following, but who will fail, due to inability to communicate in a way people understand and respond to. A person with such numbers would be well advised to put any idea of public acclaim out of his mind, directing his energies to what he can do well, otherwise he is likely to end hopelessly frustrated.

4

In the Land

The same stress line weighted in 7 (upward arrow) is the classic line of farming. Here is a lifelong friend of mine who is a farmer of dairy produce and fruit in Kent:

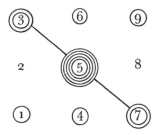

And here is his wife, who, like him, is an expert farmer:

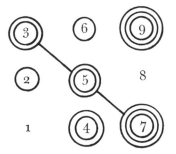

Needless to say, this is an excellent husband-and-wife team, and a happy marriage. It will be seen that the husband's stress line is balanced at either end (two rings each round 3 and 7). This is not usually a line of national leadership; the pull of practical things at soil level (7) is generally too strong. His wife has the farming line in its classic form (weighted in 7, arrow upward).

Note in both of them a full array of head numbers (3, 6, 9)—broad-minded people with wide interests, including the arts. Note that the soil numbers are represented (1, 4, 7), indicating a thorough knowledge of farming. In addition, both have all the numbers of technique and organization of material things (6, 5, 4).

The husband's very strong 5 shows, of course, that he will be successful (mastery of subject) but, moreover this 5 is so strong that it is liable to mean utterance, leadership, or co-ordination. Circumstances have not rendered this necessary to him, but it is a capacity he has in reserve. When 3 and 7 are balanced on this stress line (meaning the arrow is not headed either way), it indicates a person with great (strong 5) power of appeal, but who will remain unconscious of this, unless circumstances unexpectedly thrust it upon him and make him aware of it.

Should this ever happen to my friend, his appeal to people would be statesmanly rather than political (absence of 2 and 8, with strong 5). You would have to listen to him, otherwise he couldn't be bothered.

This is the grid of a completely relaxed man, very good at what he does, but with a hidden potential for even more, on what other people (though not he himself) would say was a larger scale. He is quite unaware of it; I have never mentioned it either to him or his wife. The slightest thing, however, could suddenly project him into public affairs in which he would be very effective. If it happened, being very relaxed, he would find it a nuisance but would do it.

I have explained this grid because this particular friend of mine, and this particular line (arrow unweighted either way), demonstrate the basic fact that a grid is a potential. Being numerical, it promises nothing. It simply indicates that *if* certain circumstances should arise, *then*....*

My friend's wife is not inclined to take risks (absence of

---

* Napoléon, by his personal name only, which he used as Emperor, had this line. As a young man, he was utterly unaware of his capacity of leadership and appeal, until time after time, circumstances placed the fact in his hands, leaving him with virtually no alternative.

8, a woman's risk number), and as her strong 7 shows, it is she who is more concerned with the day-to-day running of the farm, her husband being more an 'outside' person. Her strong 9 shows she is better at handling money than he is, though on her own she would not be a good manager (absence of 1 in relation to 9).

Now, take a careful look at this one:

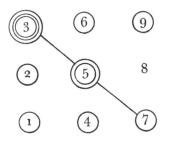

It looks like the beginnings of another national leader, does it not? And so it might prove to be, were it a man. But it is not; it is a woman—a lady who owns and runs a large wheat and livestock farm in Berkshire, employing quite a number of men.

The reader will immediately note the perfect balance of the soil numbers (1, 4, 7, each with one ring around it), meaning exceptionally balanced knowledge of people and the soil. Then, complete head numbers (3, 6, 9), with a strong 3 on the stress line, meaning that she has the gift of exercising authority over men without making them feel small.

Broad-minded and very independent (3, 6, 9), interested in literature and the arts (1, 2, 3), and with a grasp of technique, machinery and costing (4, 5, 6 respectively), she is an excellent financial manager (1 and 9 equally balanced *off* a stress line).

One sees here how, in the case of an independent woman farmer, the farming line reverses itself. Had she the line in its classic form (arrow upward), she would not be able to manage so well on her own, in that her 7 would be strong, and men as a general rule will not accept orders from a woman with strong soil numbers; she gets on the wrong side of them.

5
With a Cross to Bear

Next, multiple stress lines. Here is a man:

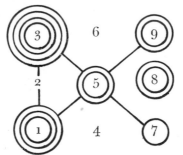

Three stress lines operate here simultaneously. He has 1 to 9, the line of worldly success, or creating something out of nothing; and 3 to 7 with a downward arrow, the leader with popular appeal. The third line, 3 to 1, whichever way it is weighted, upward or downward, is basically the same. It means dedication to a career, or talent—dedication which, in either case, is compulsive.

Let us begin by eliminating. This man is not in commerce or law (absence of 6). He has nothing to do with machinery, physics, or pure mathematics (absence of 4). He is probably a person incapable of duplicity (absence of 2), nor is he likely to be a diplomat (ditto).

He is dedicated to a career, or talent (stress line 3 to 1). If this means a career, such as in the armed forces, it looks odd that he should also have a following and popular appeal. Moreover, observe his very strong power numbers (9, 8, 7). This is not just appeal to a following; it is mass appeal. Therefore, it looks more probable that the line 3 to 1 is not dedication to a career, but to a talent.

This talent arises in 3, the number of the arts and sciences. But there is an absence of scientific principles (4) and the laws governing them (6). This narrows us down to the arts.

This is a talent connected with the arts—combined arts (3). Which?

It heads straight to 1, this talent, and with 2 (the social number) quiescent, this obviously indicates writing and new ideas, which are successfully projected (stress line 1 to 9, arrow upward) through 5 (utterance, or mastery) to 9 (power and money).

The most likely of the combined arts to head to writing on a line of dedication to a talent are music and the theatre —hardly opera, surely—in any case, the theatre in combination with something else; and he will write and think out new ideas for it. These will be very successful, causing him to have mass appeal, as well as money. He will also—note reliable 8 with two rings round it—be extremely consistent. This talent will be expressed at a consistently high level, in terms of artistic standards.

It is a person who is a star-turn of some kind, who once he achieves stardom (with those power numbers it will be big) will keep it for life.

This is obviously a star, as one looks at it more carefully. Let us say that the problem of combined arts might mean the movies, i.e. the theatre combined with photography. It doesn't sound at all like an actor. He writes or devises his own material, which no ordinary film actor does.

Yet he has mass appeal. Therefore, presumably he *must* appear. This is a strange kind of movie actor who writes his own material. The material is successfully projected (stress line 1 to 9) on a wide scale (power numbers), while the actor himself has (line 3 to 7, plus power numbers) an enormous following.

So far so good.

But there is something wrong with this assessment.

Observe how lines 3 to 7 and 1 to 9 cross each other at a right angle, thereby sealing up the mouth (5). The crossing of these two lines with that X shape means an impediment of speech. The impediment can, with weak supporting numbers, be physical. Where the supporting numbers are strong, as herein, it is unlikely to be a physical impediment. Here it means either an impediment which is imposed from within the person—a hesitancy to speak—or else an impediment which is imposed by circumstances, as in the case of a man who has taken an oath of secrecy.

This man being clearly not a diplomat, the oath of secrecy angle can be eliminated. This is someone who for some reason hesitates to speak.

Yet, if we are right about the movies, this is a star who writes his own material, and who appears in it. Does he not speak?

Well, you will have got this one long before I would, had I had this grid placed before me without knowing who it was.

It is, of course, the greatest of all movie actors, Charles Chaplin, the man who achieved world fame without speaking, and who, when the talkies were invented, *hesitated* for nearly ten years before he finally decided to speak—in *Modern Times*—and then only by singing a song with meaningless words.

While admitting that I would have been baffled by that cross over the 5—the impediment (it seems to stand in such complete contradiction to everything else)—I trust the reader may be in a mood to agree that it is remarkable how close one can come to identification in Chaplin's grid.

And this is not pretence. After doing many people's numbers, you will find yourself developing the same technique of looking at grids. It is similar to people who are adept at doing crossword puzzles; one develops an instinct for it. It is simply logic applied to numbers.

Remember, too, that we have not yet even brought Chaplin's three basic numbers into play. These reinforce what is already on the grid. By birth (16 April 1889) a 9, meaning he will bring power to whatever he does, his name is a 3, meaning his balancer is another 3, making it more certain than ever that this is someone who will achieve success in one of the combined arts, provided he plays his numbers right.

And this last brings out another important point. A

person can have the best success numbers in the world; but if he does not play them well, he can just as easily remain in square one, or reach the top and fall off. Not even the strongest numbers of a national leader (line 3 to 7) can save him from downfall or disgrace if he betrays his people's confidence (7). Numbers indicate what a person is capable of doing. There remains the question: will he?

Had I been born in the last century, and had Charles Chaplin come to me for advice as a boy, and told me of his interest in the performing arts, I would have foretold a great worldly success for him, and counselled him always to write his own material, since in this would lie his strength.

But I would have been deeply worried about that cross over the 5. Could it mean that he had to be very careful of his throat and vocal cords? Could it mean personal shyness, which he would have to master in his professional interests? Or could it mean that he would be best at dumb parts, like some clowns? Or as an acrobat? I would be obliged to say that I felt sure he would succeed, but that I could not see how.

I mention this because the right-angle cross over 5 is one of the most difficult things to determine in numerology. Where a cross occurs at an acute angle, it usually means simply a person who does not care for public speaking. The right-angle cross, meaning an impediment or obstacle, nearly always comes from deep *within* the person concerned, making it almost impossible to know what to say.

Chaplin converted it into an attribute. By playing the whole world's 'little man', without language, he became the one truly universal star of the screen.

It is not every man, however, who can cope with this impediment so brilliantly. Look for a moment at Lawrence of Arabia:

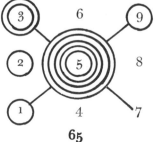

Known by almost everyone simply as Lawrence, this is an instance where one uses initials only, as he signed himself: T. E. Lawrence.

In Lawrence's grid one sees a person of immense potential political influence (5). But it is cancelled, almost like a mark of doom. He has every possibility of worldly success (stress line 1 to 9), though this line being evenly balanced at both ends (one ring each round 1 and 9), this is a person inwardly unsure of himself, troubled by conscience, or given to much self-examination.

(When *not* on a stress line, an evenly balanced 1 and 9 indicates someone who is good at financial planning.)

Then (stress line 3 to 7) he seems to have the makings of a national leader. Yet note how the line does not reach the people—his 7 is naked; it lacks arrival. And across it all lies that terrible mark of cancellation, which comes from *within*.

Lawrence was a man who could win kings and armies; yet there was something in him which was so self-enclosed that he came near to shunning humanity. He threw away worldly success; he even threw away his name. He seemed to desire annihilation. And this was of his own making, coming from within himself.

This is the meaning of that cross.

6

Utterly on One's Own

Having observed the stress line 3 to 1 in a multiple grid, we must now observe it on its own—dedication to a career, or talent.

Here is a woman—and incidentally, when studying grids blind, like this, it is essential to be told first whether it is a man or a woman. As was noted earlier, the numbers behave slightly differently for the two sexes.

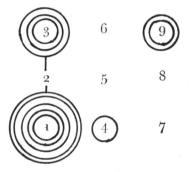

This is a woman single-mindedly dedicated to a career, or talent, to the exclusion of almost everything else (so many naked numbers). This talent, or career, arises in 1.

It is not a writer. A writer needs more clothed numbers than this, giving her more breadth of experience and understanding of others. There are not enough technical numbers (absence of 5 and 6) for it to be invention, while new ideas (1) require 5 (utterance), and 5 is naked. Whatever it is, she will make money (9), though without worrying much about it. What is really important to her is her talent, or career.

The stress line lying along the numbers of the arts and

sciences (3, 2, 1), and this being a woman, it would seem that her talent or career has something to do with the arts. Could that 4 provide a clue? In a person with so few clothed numbers as this, every number which is represented bears more weight than in the case of a person whose numbers are well spread across the grid. We observed this earlier in Sir James Jeans. What does this 4 mean?

We have already ruled out science and technology (4). The absence of the other soil number, 7, suggests a tireless person, and one who may not care much for public opinion (7), someone with technical competence (4), and of course supremely self-confident in her talent (stress line 1 to 3).

With a complete absence of heart numbers (2, 5, 8), that 4 in relation to 1 seems to mean someone who is rather earthy, and who will probably worry about her health or her diet (4—central stomach number—who worries about ailments). It shows that this talent of hers must be somehow connected with her body. Surely it means a voice. And since it communicates directly to 3, the world of the combined arts, must it not be an opera singer?

It is, of course, the greatest *diva* of our times, Maria Callas. And note the significance of that small 4: the wonderful earthy quality of her performances, which made her Tosca, for example, quite unlike anything ever heard before.

Here is one more, this time a man:

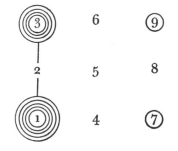

This is definitely not dedication to a career, as in the armed forces or diplomacy. There are too many naked numbers, and a total lack of organizational ability, either of people (central horizontal) or things (central vertical). It means single-minded dedication to a supreme talent. This talent arises in 1 (stronger than 3, arrow upward), from the soil. What kind of talent is it?

Like Callas, here is someone of supreme self-confidence, dedicated to his talent to the exclusion of nearly everything else. He will make money (9), and he will almost certainly be popular (7) and pay attention to public opinion.

Remembering that with grids as naked as this, the smallest thing counts, one observes that this man has one of the soil numbers missing (4), though, in a sparse grid, he has the other two (1 and 7). This means he does not have to worry about his health (4, the worrier about ailments).

Yet surely it means more than this. It must mean he has a good physique, because in a man dedicated to a talent, and with so conspicuous an absence of the wherewithal to pursue a career, what is there left but physique?

It could, I suppose, be an operatic bass of tremendous physical stature. Yet in a man (though not in a woman) one would expect to find either 5 (utterance) or 4 (technique) represented; and in this case both are naked. We are reduced to concluding that it must be an athlete, yet an athlete with some kind of artistry (3) about him.

This is the ex-world heavyweight boxing champion, Cassius Clay, under the name by which he achieved fame.

7

At a Mixed Reception

I will now demonstrate the remaining stress lines. First, the central vertical:

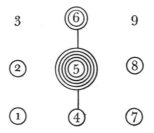

This is the line of mastery of material things or affairs, and people with this line usually convey to others an air of mastery. This inspires confidence in all save those who dislike mastery being so obvious, in whom it inspires resentment. It is the classic line of generalship.

With a weak or naked 5, it means a person who conveys an air of mastery, though without real foundation for it—unless a weak 5 (say, one ring) is in perfect balance with 6 and 4, making the line strong.

The air of mastery was particularly noticeable in this instance, the grid above being that of President John F. Kennedy.

The reader conversant with the previous chapters will be able to interpret much of this powerful and beautifully balanced grid. Let me draw attention simply to a few details.

2 and 8 in balance, with a strong 5 between, is a man capable of giving orders in a balanced way, which others can

see is fair. This is supplemented by perfect balance on the numbers of the people (1, 4, 7), the whole indicating extraordinary understanding and empathy.

3 and 9 being missing among the head numbers indicates concentration on specific issues, connected (line 6 to 4) with material matters—in this case, *inter alia*, determination that man reach the moon, and in putting the American economy on a footing which gave it the greatest growth rate it has ever experienced.

But perfect balance on 1 to 7, plus balance on 2 and 8, takes it further than this. This grid is intensely radical. If it were a general, he would not only be a brilliant operator in the field, but famous for his attention to the welfare of his men and (these days) their families. If it were an architect on the grand scale, his houses designed for the poorest families would be, like his grander houses, wonderfully thought out, and ideal to live in.

This is a mind which goes straight to fundamentals (stress line 6 to 4, weighted in 6, the brains), supported by heart balance (2 and 8) and detailed understanding (perfect balance on 1, 4, 7). In public affairs, few men can have a better grid than this.

With numbers as strong as this, absence of 9 (money), especially when allied to a balanced 8 and 7 (numbers of power), indicates someone with no need to worry about money, and who seldom actually handles it.

Here is the line of mastery again:

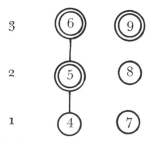

This is the grid of Henry Ford, who conveyed an air of mastery, and was in addition a veritable master of material things. This is a short name, thus each ring has more weight. Note the strong support he has in his power numbers

(9, 8, 7)—in his case, engines (power), money and influence. Ford's influence on the world was decisive. Horizontally, observe his strong brains (balanced, in doubles), two numbers of the heart, and two balanced numbers of the people. Behind his practical application (line 6 to 4) lay the dreamer (strong 9 and 6) who wanted (5, 8, the heart) everyone (4, 7, the people) to have a car.

Note also the absence of the numbers of the arts. 'History is bunk,' quoth he.

This same line, in the realm of thought, indicates materialism (organization of material things, mentally). Here it is in one of the foremost materialist thinkers of this century, Sigmund Freud, the proponent of psychoanalysis:

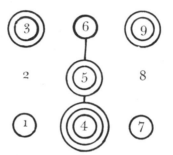

Note the powerful mind, with 3 and 9 balanced in doubles, and another balance in 1 and 7, in the numbers of people. The air of mastery (line 4 to 6) of course surrounded Freud, with all three numbers clothed. But note in particular the stress on 4, the number of neurosis, on which his life's work was based; and remember that throughout much of his life he worried (4), and with reason, about his health.

Next, the line 9 to 7:

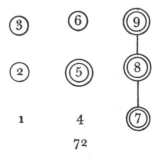

This line means dedication to a cause, or to a gift. It is the foremost line of an influencer. As with stress line 3 to 1 (dedication to a career, or talent), so with this. In a person with strong numbers, dedication is a compulsive urge. It is not dictated by financial necessity.

Due to the letters contained in line 9 to 7, with only one vowel, this line is comparatively rare. It is a line of power (9, 8, 7, the power numbers), and here it is shown with perfect balance, in doubles, indicating dedication of a kind capable of influencing on a general scale. (Put simply, perfect balance in these three numbers means influencing the nation.)

This is the grid of Quintin Hogg, founder of the London Polytechnic, the successful London businessman who devoted his life to the cause of education for the underprivileged, and whose work and achievement ultimately brought about, on more than a national scale, a revolutionary change of attitude towards education.

A wonderfully balanced grid, the absence of 1 (self), combined with absence of 4, with all the other numbers clothed, means a selfless person, for whom achievement of object is all-important.

Perhaps the supreme example of this line as dedication to a cause is Giuseppe Mazzini, the 'soul' of the Italian Risorgimento.

Here is the same line in dedication to a gift—in this case, the gift of healing:

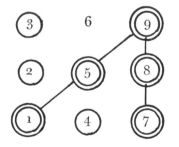

Again, with perfect balance on 9 to 7, meaning the capacity to exercise general influence, together with perfect balance on stress line 1 to 9, meaning a person who escapes immaturity, with wonderfully well balanced numbers, and two lines concentrating in 9 (power), this is the grid of the American healer Phineas Quimby, who believed he had accidentally stumbled on the secret of Jesus' healing powers, and who is usually regarded as the father of the movement which became known as New Thought.

Turning now to the line of the reformers, here is the foremost man of the age, the Mahatma, known throughout his life by his surname only, and who signed himself M. K. Gandhi: *

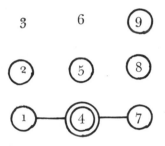

Reformers, in the sense of people who fundamentally seek to alter and improve things for the people, belong on the line of the people (1 to 7). They operate usually from 1 (ideas), through 4 (fundamentals), to 7 (food). In the case of a religious reformer, which Gandhi was not, 7 means spiritual food. However they are, there is a religious quotient in reformers of this type.

Remember in the above grid that this is a short name, therefore all the rings are stronger.

Observe in Gandhi's grid three perfect balances without impediment—along 9 to 7, capacity to influence the nation; along 2 to 8, the perfectly balanced heart; and along 1 to 9, unusual skill in propaganda and fund-raising.

Note the heavy 4: fussiness about food—he was so fussy about milk he travelled everywhere with his own goat— and domestic routine. When in his *ashram*, he slept and woke at exactly the same moment each day (his waking—

---

* Those of us who knew him called him Bapu or, in front of other people, Mahatmaji.

at 4 a.m.—was almost uncanny), and his entire day was organized as a routine. Unbelievably clever at dealing with people (perfect balance 2 to 8), his organization in material matters (central vertical) was impeded by inability to grasp financial angles (absence of 6), despite his genius for fund raising (perfect balance 1 to 9 *not* on a stress line), for which history affords no comparison.

With only one head number (9), his leadership was devoted to specific objects concerned with power (9)—independence for India, the removal of untouchability (power, human rights). He seldom concerned himself with the arts, education or learning (absence of 3) and had no love of fine things (absence of 6). His favoured *modus operandi* was judicious breaking of the law (absence of 6), such as when he picked up salt on Dandi beach. His outward emblem was spinning—4, the central number of manual labour—which he practised each day, if possible.

Here is the same line in a religious reformer, Mary Baker Eddy, founder of the Church of Christ Scientist:

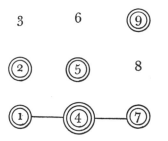

Observe 1 and 7 in balance: ideas and food (7, agriculture), meaning spiritual food. Also, perfect balance on 1 to 9 *not* on a stress line, and in doubles, meaning exceptional ability in propaganda, fund-raising and handling public or organizational money, though quite uninterested in money in respect of herself (absence of 6 and 8, commerce and banking). Mrs. Eddy's remarkable record in founding newspapers (perfect balance on 1 to 9) has its memorial today in the *Christian Science Monitor*.

Reformers are also pioneers; and particularly where

women are concerned, the line sometimes means more a pioneer than a reformer, though of course there are similar elements in both.

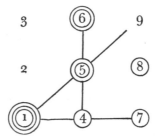

This is the grid of Amy Johnson, the first woman to fly solo from Australia to Britain—in a single-engined aircraft, remember, one of the bravest women in the world.

Here one sees the line of the pioneer (1 to 7, typically weighted in 1, ideas), well balanced with technical mastery (line 6 to 4, weighted in 6, the brain) with the line of worldly success (1 to 9), though with no desire to achieve power (absence of 9 on a stress line)—the person who does something because it is worth it.

The cross over 5 (the mouth) at this (acute) angle means dislike of public speaking.

I remember as a little boy listening in on the radio (itself still an exciting novelty) to the arrival of Amy Johnson in her plane, at the conclusion of her momentous journey. Then and there, she was interviewed. It was about the worst interview I have ever heard. In her voice, you could hear her incomprehension that anyone should wish to hear her say anything.

Why talk? She had *done* it.

Sometimes it happens that a person with this line, carried away by other talents or interests, does not exercise it in its reforming and pioneering capacity. Where this happens, the affects are adverse. There is a peculiar quality about this line which demands that it be used.

Here, as an illustration of this, is the grid of one of the best-loved film stars any of us can remember, Judy Garland:

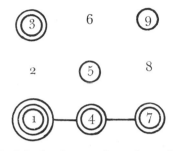

By her delightful singing and acting, she gave pleasure to millions; but it would be difficult to imagine a more unhappy personal life, tormented by instability, at the root of which lay denial, or imperception, of the often unglamorous yet rewarding qualities of this stress line.

Of the many great men who have had this line, the one who most completely combined in his character the line's two qualities of pioneer and reformer, with the line's slightly religious quality, was Vasco da Gama, discoverer of the sea route to India.

Next, the central horizontal:

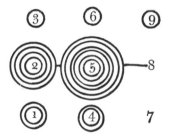

This is the line of service to others, the line of the heart. Whether as an employer, a colleague, or a subordinate, people with this line are at their best when serving others, and they usually know how to organize other people without upsetting them. For this line to signify a successful employer-organizer, as opposed to a subordinate, perfect balance is required somewhere on the grid, preferably on the cerebral line (3, 6, 9), as above, or on the line of the people (1, 4, 7).

The grid above, denoting organization on the grand scale, is that of one of the most capable and admired women of this century, the late Edwina Mountbatten, the keynote of whose immensely active life was service to others.

Observe here 2 in its aspect of strength in a woman, and the very large 5, denoting complete mastery of subject. Also, perfect balance of the head numbers, a major asset in a woman who is required to exercise authority. Note, too, the character of her work—2 and 5, with absence of 8: civil.

Though this line, being administrative and organizational, is typically related to work in connection with other people, it can equally indicate someone working on their own. Here is my Chinese dentist in Hongkong:

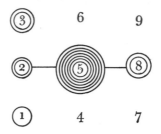

The keynote of a dentist's and a doctor's life is service to others, and note how both surgery (2) and medicine (8) occur on this line. Observe in this grid how absolute mastery of subject (5) is combined with artistry (all the arts numbers represented, with a good 3, demonstrative science). This is a dental surgeon who is a consummate artist. Note finally the most intriguing aspect of absence of 9 (money). Except when crossing the ferry between Hongkong and Kowloon, he never handles it. This meaning of absence of 9 only occurs with strong numbers, in particular 5, with 8 clothed.

Here now is the cerebral line:

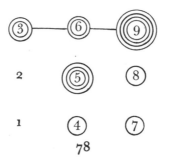

This line means sureness of idea. People who have it convey a sense of remoteness from others, and they are not given to humour or wit. Though inwardly they are often tense, outwardly they are calm. To an unusual degree, they know exactly what they wish to achieve, and how to do it (the brain). They are admired and respected at a distance, but only a select few can come close to their remoteness. In such as can, they can inspire deep affection.

The grid above is that of the composer Frédéric Chopin. Others who had this line include John Churchill, first Duke of Marlborough, Sir Stamford Raffles, founder of Singapore, John D. Rockefeller, Giacomo Puccini and Columbus (equally as Cristoforo Colombo and Cristóbal Colón). All had the characteristics stated above.

Finally, there are the four diagonals.

The line 6 to 8, however it is weighted, means a capacity for partnership between equals, the strongest of partnerships.

The line 2 to 6 means a capacity for partnership between two who are not equally endowed or talented, 6 being stronger than 2.

The line 4 to 8, when weighted in 4, indicates ability to work faithfully and undemandingly for an organization or an individual, often on confidential matters. Weighted in 8, it indicates ability to inspire confidence (8, trust) in such a person working for one.

Line 2 to 4, however weighted, need not be a difficult line, but it often is. Where it connects technique (4) with duplicity (2), it has a criminal tendency, or does not get far due simply to being too clever. Where it connects emotion and passion (2) with neurosis (4), it is either cruel or neurotic, and in either case is difficult to live with.

The diagonals occur mainly when doing grids of the personal name only; and the reader will recall that this was how I advised beginning, when doing the numbers of an unmarried girl.

Where a man is concerned, especially when one is in a quandary over his numbers, it sometimes helps to do a grid of his personal name only, to see how it confirms or conflicts with his full name grid.

79

Personal name grids are used when giving advice on marriage. But it is unwise to advise on this, unless a girl asks about a specific person, giving his name and date of birth. By doing his numbers first, then the girl's—doing first her personal name grid, then a grid with her name as it would be with her husband's surname added—it is possible to advise.

Since, however, by this stage of the proceedings, she is usually determined to marry the man anyway, in practice it is a waste of time.

8

With Female Stars Present

Most women change their names on marriage. Dealing with this could be called advanced-level numerology, really deserving of a book to itself. Merely as an introduction to the subject, I propose in this chapter to illustrate two instances of what happens when the name changes.

In order to make this understandable, let me first illuminate the meaning of two stress lines, in respect of women, taking as examples two of the most famous actresses of an earlier generation.

Here, first, is the grid of the greatest actress of her age, Sarah Bernhardt, the Divine Sarah:

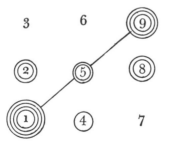

Note first—though this is not the main point I wish to make—perfect balance of the heart numbers (2, 5, 8), and in doubles. In an actress, this means a marvellous control of the expression of the emotions.

Now, to the point.

This stress line 1 to 9, the line of worldly success, or

creating something out of nothing, is in some ways a man's line. Whether as a man or a woman, this line, weighted in 1, indicates someone who is going places, and in their own way. Fine in a man, but difficult in a woman, if she wants to have any kind of domestic life.

A woman with this line in a strong grid, which this is, either desires, or will have, a career of her own; and if she has, her career comes first, domestic life being an adjunct, as it is in a man.

Marriage to a woman of this kind is difficult. It can only work where the husband is richer and more secure than she, and enjoys having a career wife—rare. Even then, it is useless to pretend she can look after him as a wife. Her only course is to abandon all pretence on this matter, and ensure that her husband has first-class domestic servants, who can run his home perfectly for him. This seldom happens. Sarah Bernhardt's marriage was a domestic disaster.

The character of this stress line shows up in the parts for which Bernhardt was famous. She played empresses and queens—anything in heroic mould—and in some of her greatest performances she played a man: Maeterlinck's Pelléas, in Rostand's *L'Aiglon*, and as Hamlet.

Now here, by contrast, from the English stage, is Ellen Terry:

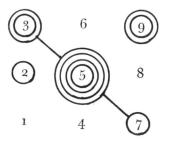

This stress line, because it heads direct to 7 (the influence of the masses), and 7 is clothed, is a line of appeal. It is the heart-throb, the ideal woman, the lovely heroine.

Ellen Terry was hopeless with money, of course (absence of 6 and 8, commerce and banking). Contrast Bernhardt's powerful 1 (literature) with Ellen Terry's lack of it. Bernhardt was literary. She could conduct a conversation in rhyming alexandrines, making them up as she went along. It is doubtful whether Ellen Terry knew a good play from a bad one (though she probably thought she did). She simply did what Irving told her, and to perfection. Also—rare in an actress—she was completely unselfish (absence of 1 and 4, with 7 clothed).

Once again, the character of this stress line shows up in the parts for which Ellen Terry was famous. Where Sarah Bernhardt conveyed a sense of beholding the incomparable, and lived in people's minds as Phèdre or Andromaque, Ellen Terry conveyed a sense of beholding a vision of beauty and lived in people's minds as Portia and Juliet.

There was once a girl called Annie Wood. By name she is a 1, and Annie is a 7, both of them soil numbers, indicating basic problems for husbands.

She was born on 1 October 1847, which is a 4 (another soil number, the fundamentalist who sees the word mother as motherhood). The date is made up of 1—1—2 (becoming rather formidable by this time, with ever more soil numbers). Her balancer (1 + 4) is 5, an organizer. I refrain from comment.

On the grid she appears thus:

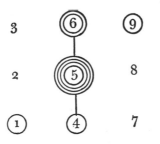

She has the line of mastery of material affairs, and conveys an air of mastery, not especially likeable in a young lady with so many off-grid soil numbers. With 5 as balancer, all told, a little too managerial.

But there is hope. In the realm of thought, her stress line can mean materialism, and this may act as a safe balance against those soil numbers, which might otherwise lead to religiosity.

Balanced it all was, for a time. So much so, in fact, that at the age of twenty-one, she married that most balanced of religious persons, an Anglican clergyman.

His name was Frank Besant. Overnight, Annie Wood found she had another name.

As **Annie Besant**, she had become 9, a name of power; while her balancer had changed from 5 to 4, the fundamental, the universal.

This was difficult enough. Worse, from her husband's point of view, was this:

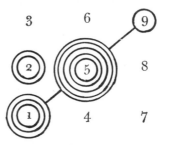

She was now set for a career of her own, with increased power of utterance, and a name of power. In a short time, the whole world knew it.

To start with, she went off at a tangent. Still thinking in terms of her line of materialism, which she had in fact lost —even to the extent of her 6 and 4 being grid-naked—this Anglican clergyman's wife became an atheist. She became, indeed, the world's leading lady atheist. In addition, she became the foremost protagonist of birth control, and a formidable advocate of free speech on matters then considered unmentionable. She was dubbed obscene. There was a moment when the genteel came close to seeing her as the Female Anti-Christ. Politically, she was so radical that even Bernard Shaw became concerned, and tried to reason her into moderation—to no avail.

Her marriage lasted—her poor husband—for seven years. When it broke up, she kept her name, as well as her married style. Never mind what happened to her husband—no one,

without research, can remember what happened to him—
she was Mrs. Besant, a married woman, publicly the most
formidable (note her numbers of masterful women, in addition to 9 by name) woman of her day.

Then, in her late thirties, she suddenly made the most
sensational personal *volte-face* of any famous woman of the
nineteenth century. She read *The Secret Doctrine*, by
Helena Blavatsky, and was converted to the esoteric. To the
astonishment of all grave materialists, she in due course
announced the identification of her previous incarnations
—all of them rather grand ones, nothing about Annie
Besant being in half-measures.

Actually, in Blavatsky, she had stumbled upon the reality
of her new set of numbers—herself as she now was, but as
she had not been prior to marriage. She was now on course
—and, with reference to *volte-faces* such as this, remember,
in relation to her numbers as a whole, under either name,
her repetitive 1.

After much travel, she finally settled in India, where she
became not only head (line 1 to 9, someone going to the top,
with two 4s, the universal, and a name of power) of the
Theosophical Society, but the foremost champion (formula
repeated) of Indian home rule, the person who, so far as an
Englishwoman possibly could in such extraordinary circumstances, prepared the political way for the Mahatma,
who superseded her.

It is always easier to demonstrate through the extraordinary, since in such people the characteristics show forth
more plainly. Annie Besant stands among women as utterly
remarkable, of immense influence. Her life is one of the
most extraordinary ever lived.

The other most extraordinary life in our times is that of
the little girl who, aged four, had her name gleaming in the
night sky of thousands of cities all over the world, the neon
letters sometimes several feet high, much larger than those
of the world-famous adults with whom she was appearing
in the same movie.

No more extraordinary conditions could be imagined for
a woman than those which surrounded the childhood of
Shirley Temple. Here she is:

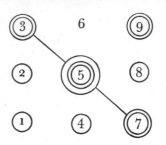

Where Annie Besant had the stress line of Sarah Bernhardt, the heroic, Shirley Temple has the line of Ellen Terry, the ideal, the heart-throb. 3 and 7 in balance, with a larger 5, means someone who, unless circumstances allow, remains unaware of her capacity to touch the heart. With those power numbers (all present, with 9 and 7 balanced) it would mean mass appeal if she did; yet with this balance between 3 and 7 there is no leaning toward exposition.

In Shirley Temple's case, it would probably be true to say that, even when playing with Fred Astaire and Ginger Rogers, the top stars of the time, she was in general unaware of quite how great a star she was. As a world figure in entertainment, she was only outrivalled by Chaplin, after all.

I shall not do these numbers in detail. The grids are so clear, they explain themselves.

The child darling of the movies was wisely withdrawn from public life at a suitable moment, grew up in (relative) tranquillity, and in due course got married.

Years, however, had not dimmed her fame. For her to have dropped one of her names on marriage would have been a physical impossibility. A new generation thus encountered Mrs. Shirley Temple Black.

And behold the astonishing thing that happened:

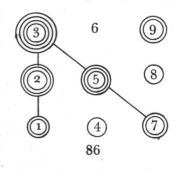

By a miracle (of marriage) she retained her line of popular appeal (3 to 7), indeed strengthened it, her 3 now being stronger, and *conscious* of appeal, meaning she is no longer indifferent to making use of it; while at the same time she acquired an additional stress line (3 to 1, dedication to a career)—in her case, public service. This line is weighted in 3, indicating administrative ability. It is on very strong cultural numbers, the meaning of which, in a public personality, we saw in Lee Kuan Yew. In addition, the numbers of the people are also strengthened (1 and 7 balanced).

When she was a little girl, everyone said, 'But whatever will become of her when she grows up?' Well, this is what did. Her numbers are in every way stronger now than when she was a child.

And note those strong numbers on the line 1 to 9, when *not* on a stress line. No one better could be thought of for a fund-raising campaign (1 and 9 in balance). Her name would be enough, of course. But with her, there is in addition, dedication, ability and understanding.

Shirley Temple was a 5 by name. Shirley Temple Black is a 7. In describing 7 as a woman, I explained the difficulties, and the importance of having outside interests. This is a perfect example of what a woman 7 can achieve and be, when she lives her life somewhat in public, keeping dreams out of the way. She thus becomes a balanced 7—see the description of 7 as a man—steady, equable and the maker of a happy home.

Remarkable numbers—of a person for whom admiration (line 3 to 7) will not diminish.

9
Take Warning

Here are some caveats.

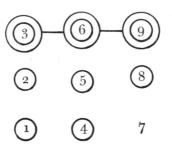

This man has the line of sureness of idea. He will be remote from others, not given to wit. He will be respected at a distance. He will inspire affection only in those few who can penetrate his remoteness.

But this is the cerebral line in perfect balance and in doubles. We observed some of its problems before, in Francis Bacon. Being here, in addition, the stress line, it is not simply overwhelmingly strong. It is appalling.

Beneath it is another line of perfect balance in the heart numbers (2, 5, 8), meaning a man who is a genius in dealing with people—we observed it in Gandhi. Such a combination of these two perfect balances would seem unbelievable, had it not occurred.

Beneath this are two balanced numbers of the people, with 7 missing. On this grid, which is of gigantic strength, this means complete understanding of what people need, coupled with (absence of 7) not simply tirelessness, but an energy and dynamism almost passing belief.

This is a grid of such genius and perfection as to be more than a human being can carry within himself. Being too large, these numbers will end either in lunacy, or in some terrible distortion of intent. They are simply too much, too strong.

This is the grid of Adolf Hitler.

Here is another:

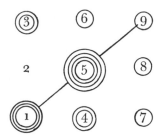

This is a man. He has the line of worldly success. He has good cerebral numbers (3, 6, 9), and all the numbers of the people (1, 4, 7). He has perfect balance in the numbers of power (9, 8, 7), indicating a desire or capacity to influence the nation. He has technical understanding (6, 5, 4, all represented). He is incapable of duplicity (absence of 2), a man's man (5 and 8, with absence of 2).

Men with this stress line are out for themselves. Making something out of nothing, they are compelled to be so. This is not the kind of personality whom people will accept as a great general influencer, though they will happily accept him as himself, an individual who contributes something.

For this reason, perfect balance on 9 to 7, when occurring with a 1 to 9 stress line, is liable to be a cause of frustration. The man will have a desperate urge to achieve more than people are willing to accept. Born in a high level of society, a man can usually manage this, converting it to other channels of energy. A man less favourably born will have difficulty. His individual ideas (strong 1) are liable to be spurned or ridiculed by those among whom he finds him-self, being beyond them. This scorn will feed frustration, leading in extreme circumstances to abnormality.

This was true of the man of this grid. Warped by disinclination of others to listen to him, he took his own way to the top (line 1 to 9), and did, indeed, achieve something which influenced the nation.

It is the grid of Lee Harvey Oswald, the assassin of President Kennedy.

The caveat here is this: If you wish to give sound advice by means of numerology, it is preferable to meet the person first, or in the case of an infant, to meet the parents, in order to know from what position in society one is starting.

Here is a last one, a young man whose numbers I did recently in India:

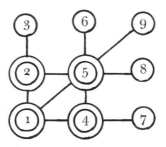

This is another instance of a grid containing too much: perfect balance on both the cerebral and the power numbers, and five stress lines.

This, however, is not the grid of an explosive or dangerous person. Here the multiplicity of stress lines is having the effect of lessening the intensity of each. In one respect, this is to his advantage, because he has the central vertical and horizontal cross over 5.

This cross indicates a streak of the self-destructive. A person with this cross on its own can be highly talented (the cross covers all the organizational numbers), but either because he has a vile temper, or cannot see reason, or acts in a contradictory manner, he will have difficulty in putting his talents to good use. In this instance, the cross is favourably modified by the line of dedication to a career (1 to 3), making it less of a problem.

The advice I gave this young man was this:

In the years ahead he will probably acquire a good deal of general knowledge, together with technical competence, possibly in more than one line of activity; and he will wish to put this to independent use, feeling he can go far if he does. Others are liable to be impressed by his knowledge and competence, and may urge him to set up his own business, or engage in some independent enterprise. They may be prepared even to finance him.

If he takes this line, his chances of success are minimal. He will need to resist the urgings of others, and of himself, in this respect. His security lies in being a reliable employee, capable of putting his hand competently to a fairly wide range of matters.

There is one final caveat: Never change your name, in the hope of obtaining more favourable numbers. If you are a woman, your numbers will change anyway on marriage, and this is difficult enough.* Do not make it more difficult than it need be.

Numerology is simply arithmetic in another guise. Feed it into a computer, and with correct programming, the machine would instantly issue accurate character readings.† It would also, with similar accuracy, predict—as we do when looking at statistics. Your numbers *are* your statistics.

Deliberately change your name, and the computer would issue the character of a slightly different person. But you remain *you*. All you have done, therefore, is to give yourself a name which is not quite *you*, which is a nuisance and pointless.

Our names, in whatever land, are given to us by either our father or our grandfather. Our name is their will.

This is something which lies beyond arithmetic.

Look again at the proverb on the title page of this book.

---

* The change of numbers on marriage simply reflects an actuality. You leave one house and family, and enter another. Numbers convey implacable truth.

† I would not advise trying this, however. I suspect the readings would come forth as a series of maledictions, the machine not having the numerologist there to soften the blow. Grids contain a great deal, far more than is in these pages. When doing a person's numbers, one tells them only certain selected things, giving encouragement or warning. The rest is best left unsaid. Numerals have no conscience.

10

Be a Man

When doing numerology, one quickly becomes aware how few are the people who have strong grids. In the course of a year of doing people's numbers, one is more conscious of defects, difficulties and disappointments than of gifts, wisdom and strength.

The world being what it is, this is inevitable.

Because of this, it is important to know what a really strong grid looks like—to use as a point of comparison. Otherwise, one finds oneself giving advice to people in a way which over-strengthens their confidence, sometimes causing them to act rashly.

Among the strongest of grids are those of naval or military commanders. More than any men on earth, they need strength. By comparison with a general, a politician, however gifted, is a small man. It is battle, whether we like it or not, which decides the fate of nations.

There are three lines of generalship. The classic is 6 to 4, the commander (the human body) in the field. Among World War II generals, Field Marshal Montgomery of Alamein has this line. Fully clothed (6, 5, 4 covered), and with strong support in other numbers, it is the line which is surest of victory.

Next is line 3 to 1, dedication to a career. This is the general who, because it is known he is dedicated to a career, will be asked to perform the impossible. Often, men with this line are aware of this. When they are, they are particularly able, their ideas being based on a certainty of shortages.

Wavell—'The only British general who showed a touch of genius was Wavell,' as his great German adversary,

Rommel, said of him—has this line. So too Lord Mount-batten, sent to Asia to supreme command of the impossible (he is a 1 by balancer, double 5 by name and birth), and who converted it into complete victory, of mind as well as limbs.

The third line is 1 to 9, the man usually described as a political or diplomatic general—the man who, while having to direct in the field, is required to be adept at dealing with international military alliances. A perfect example of a general with this line was Dwight D. Eisenhower.

I have already shown several strong grids, of which the strongest was probably that of the late President Kennedy. I shall now show one which is even stronger, and explain briefly how this particular man used the qualities in it.

For this purpose, I shall once more summon up someone from the past, this time the greatest figure in European military history, usually accounted one of the five greatest generals who have ever lived—Prince Eugène.

Though, throughout his career, Eugène was associated with Vienna—where he was known in German as Prinz Eugen—and though he spoke several languages, he thought in French. Regardless of what language he might be writing a letter in, he signed his name in French:

$$\text{EUGENE DE SAVOIE}$$
$$5\ 3\ 7\ 5\ 5\ 5 \quad 4\ 5 \quad 1\ 1\ 4\ 6\ 9\ 5$$
$$3 \qquad\quad 9 \qquad\ 8$$
$$2$$

Date of birth:

$$18\ \text{October}\ 1663$$
$$9 \qquad 1 \qquad 7$$
$$8 \qquad\qquad \text{Balancer}\ (2+8):\ 1$$

His birth number, 8, means consistency of performance, and one who inspires trust. It is made up of power (9), ideas and command (1), defence and gunnery (7).

His personality is 2, the man who has a feminine streak in him, or gentleness. The personal name, Eugène, being a 3 (number of the arts and sciences), the 1 in his birth will probably connect with literature.

His balancer is 1, the number of sole command. This, for a general, is the ideal balancer, because it is command which is ambitionless. Men in war sense this quality in a leader, and respond to it more readily than to any other form of command.

Here now, in his grid, is the Prince Eugène de Savoie:

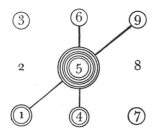

The reader will by this time, I trust, be familiar enough with this subject to share with me the gasp of wonder which this magnificent grid provokes.

Note, first, the perfect balance of the head numbers (3, 6, 9, with one ring round each), indicating absolute mastery of the mind, breadth of vision and calm. Men with these numbers in perfect balance, if they are well supported by other numbers, as in this case they are, stand out from among others by a certain inner eminence.

He has two stress lines, and both are lines of generalship.

Stress line 4 to 6, the classic line of generalship in the field, is here weighted in 4 (detail and technique) indicating, with perfect balance of the head numbers, exceptional skill at tactics.

Nearly all great generals repeat their tactics, basing these on how they achieved their first victory. It was Wellington's knowledge of Napoléon's first victories which brought about the issue of Waterloo. Napoléon, incomparably great as a civil ruler (he had 2 and 5, with absence of 8—the civil ruler—and a powerful 6, codifier of law—the Code Napoléon), repeated himself in battle—once too often.

As the lines advanced at Waterloo, Wellington could *see* what Napoléon was going to do.

94

My reader will appreciate that, in this chapter, I am dealing with some of the greatest men who have ever lived, between whom comparisons are ridiculous.

My aim here is to show a man's life, as he himself might wish it to be.

He does not wish to be assassinated (John F. Kennedy), or end his life in the remote and awful grandeur of St. Helena (Napoléon). He will wish to die peacefully, in his own home, surrounded by love, and with the sense of having achieved something.

All men desire this. Few attain it.

To show to you someone who did all of this, without a missing item in the four listed above, I have turned to Eugène.

This, in fact, is the meaning of Eugène's numbers—an utterly satisfying life, from beginning to end.

In a man, however, this means risk and an ability to accept wounds.

Few men being prepared to accept the latter, few make it.

We opened this discussion on the subject of stress line 6 to 4, weighted on 4, and on Eugène's mastery of tactics.

Eugène was renowned—and is known in every military textbook worthy of the name—as the general who never repeated his tactics, except where he saw that if he did, it would take the enemy by surprise. As a tactical general, Eugène probably stands unique in the annals of war.

Stress line 1 to 9, with a heavy 5—the political or diplomatic line of generalship—he put to brilliant use in upholding the Grand Alliance.

Note that all three numbers on line 6 to 4 are clothed.

This, whether or not on a stress line, is of advantage to a general. This line representing the human body, in a general it needs to be complete: the complete man central in the field. Many famous commanders have managed to get away with it without 6 or 4—Nelson had no 4, Wavell no 6 —but in generalship, lack of one of these numbers indicates a disability of some kind.

Eugène has all the numbers of the people (1, 4, 7), which are of course also the numbers of soldiery, manual labour and gunnery. In addition to having the number of sole command as his balancer, his 3 and 7 being balanced (one ring around each) means in addition he has unconscious appeal.

Perfect balance in the head numbers, especially with a strong 5, accentuates the content of the other numbers. With him, the soil numbers mean a person of tremendous understanding (1), practical knowledge (4), and appeal to his men (7). Added to this, his number of personality (2) is that which exercises power of attraction.

The cross over his mouth (5), being at an acute angle, means he does not care for public speaking. In that age, when generals usually addressed their troops before leading them into battle, Eugène seldom spoke. He did not have to. For his troops, the mere sight of him was enough, as he rode last into the field, usually pale as death, and curiously hunched on his horse. Seldom in war has there been a commander whose men would go forward with such confidence and sureness of renown. Never has such glory surrounded a name.*

Note that his two missing numbers, 2 and 8, are compensated for by his being a 2 by name and an 8 by birth, bringing him as near as possible to a fully clothed grid. Were the grid actually clothed in full, with numbers as strong as this it would pass the limit of the humanly bearable.

Observe his 5—immense political power, combined with the organization of armies. In this grid, marvellously balanced, everything is large-scale. The enormous central 5: and Eugène was central to a continent—apart from Louis XIV, the most decisive figure in Europe.

Note the absence of 2 and 8, in relation to a very strong 5. This is a statesman, rather than a politician. Eugène had no time for the petty wranglings and disputation involved in men's day-to-day dealings, and was not in this sense an organizer of people (absence of 2 and 8).

For this reason, coupled with the acute angle cross on 5 (unwillingness to speak) he very seldom appeared at an

---

* In whatever country, if an officer identified himself as having served on Prince Eugène's field staff, all men rose to their feet, and those in uniform saluted. There has never been anything like this in military history.

Imperial reception. If he did, he outshone the Emperor, the guests tending to surround Eugène, leaving the Emperor isolated save for his aides. When the two of them had to discuss something, they met on their own, in the Emperor's study with only the secretaries present.

Remember that the stress line 1 to 9 means creating something out of nothing. Eugène made good use of this line. Again and again, due to the ineptitude of the Imperial Court at Vienna, he was obliged to raise armies out of nothing, and money where there was seemingly none. And here note his grasp of financing armies—horizontal 6 on a perfect balance, and on a fully clothed stress line.

By virtue of this same number in a specially strong position, he was a collector and builder (6, collections and construction, the patron). As a famous print of him shows, when he entered a gallery, people fell over themselves trying to sell him works of art.

A connoisseur of books, printing and ancient manuscripts (this was where his 1, literature, came into play), he owned one of the finest private libraries in Europe. Throughout the continent he was known as the most discerning (2, personality) and munificent patron of the arts and learning.

He built the Belvedere in Vienna, and in the Little Belvedere, his home, he created the most astounding private house in Europe, an unequalled masterpiece of the sumptuous, the simple and the practical (6, love of fine things, plus 2, ditto, his name).

As he handled military finance, so did he handle his personal finances. He became very wealthy. Anything to do with banking came to him naturally—8 by birth—while his two stress lines led to 6 and 9 (calculated risk, and speculation with a calm mind—perfect balance of head numbers).

Having 1 as his balancer, 2 as his full name, and 3 as his personal name, it was, of course, virtually impossible to have friendly dealings with him as an equal.

Eugène is a particularly interesting example of a 2 by personality.

Born with a frail constitution, as a child he was so delicate that it was felt the only hope for him was to enter the Church. He forsook this idea at a fairly early age.

But at the Court of Louis XIV, his insistence on fine clothes (strongly placed 6), coupled with gentleness of manner (2, personality), led Louis to think him effeminate, a quality the king could not stand. He so contrived matters as to effect what amounted to Eugène's dismissal from Court, an action Louis was to rue for the rest of his life, and pay for in the blood of thousands of Frenchmen. For it was then that Eugène turned to Vienna.

What Louis had done, without realizing it, was to dismiss from his court a young man who was potentially—though himself unaware of this, unless circumstances should thrust it upon him (3 and 7 in balance, with large 5)—the greatest general on earth.

In subsequent years, by physical discipline Eugène completely mastered the disabilities of his frail constitution, a rare and remarkable instance of this. In battle he was wounded seventeen times, and lived to die peacefully in his bed.

Though a number of women figured in his life, he never married. He was one of those 2s who, having achieved an inner balance in the conflict this number presents, seeks the company of women, though not in marriage.*

Eugène's is the most perfect set of numbers I can think of. He had everything, and in balance; and he used what he had, all of it. The hero of some seventy battles, in most of which he was the victor; supreme tactician; sagacious statesman; constructor of fine buildings; patron of the arts and learning.

From the quietude of his library to the filth and horror of battle, this was every inch a man.

---

* In his last years, Eugène could sometimes be glimpsed through the windows of the Little Belvedere, playing chess with the lady who was his companion towards the end. I always think this is one of the most fascinating side glances in European history—a woman playing chess (tactics) with the greatest general on earth. She must have been *very* clever—the kind of woman one would love to have known.

III

WHEN THE SUN SHINES

I

On a Lion

Prediction on the basis of numbers is simply a matter of using common sense and giving advice. Years later, when one's words prove to have been true, people see them as predictions, and are apt to wonder if one is psychic. In fact, there is nothing psychic about it. It is solely a question of reading statistics correctly.

When doing the numbers of young people, who are looking ahead to the future, there is one particularly useful aid, which is like a walking stick when climbing a hill. By simple arithmetic one can tell when, in the future, the sun is going to shine on a person particularly. This is when, in the course of the century, our numbers—quite literally—come up.

Every human being is like a magnet, exercising power of attraction. There are times in our lives—when our numbers come up—when this magnetic power is stronger than usual, meaning that we attract *more*, whether it be ideas, opportunities, friends, or simply happiness.

In this and the next chapter I shall do two sets of numbers, with a view to demonstrating favourable decades.

These occur in our lives when any one of our three basic numbers appears as the decade digit of the year, viz. throughout the 1970s the decade digit is 7.

Favourable decades are times when, particularly towards the end of a decade, we either have a sense of ease, or do particularly satisfactory work, or seem to achieve things without effort. They are also times when, if at all, things unexpectedly fall into our lap, or seem to.

The only reason I can think of for favourable decades is this: If we are, for instance, by name a 2, whether we know it or not, we *are* a 2; and when a 2 decade occurs, that number is drumming at us more than usual, and for ten years. We hear it daily on the radio; it eyes us from calendars; we use it every time we date a letter. It is a time when we are particularly surrounded by that number; and being a 2, this perhaps has an effect on us.

There is something about numbers here which we simply do not understand. The foregoing is the nearest I can come to a suggestion. It is similar, on a widely extended and diffuse scale, to our birthday being *our* day.

There is no such thing as an unfavourable decade. Decades are either favourable or neutral. In a neutral decade, what we achieve is by struggle and hard work only. We must not expect things to fall into our lap.

Much depends on how old a person is when he or she experiences a favourable decade, and on whether the decades occur bunched together or isolated, having neutral decades between them. Favourable decades which come consecutively are stronger.

Here, first, is the man who was known to the whole of the theatrical profession as the Master:

NOEL COWARD

5 6 5 3 3 6 5 1 9 4
   1   1
      2

Date of birth:

16 December 1899

7   3   9

1   Balancer (2 + 1): 3

By birth he is 1 (ideas, literature, invention, sole command), and it is made up of 7 and 3, which in a man means something pleasing, or a desire to please (remember the relationship between 3 and 7 on the grid) and this will be strong (9).

In his name, 1 appears again, twice, insistently. Noel is a 1, Coward is a 1. This, with his birth numbers, is liable to mean ideas of a pleasing nature. The personality being 2 at once suggests the theatre as the arena of these ideas. This is a man who will write (1) for the theatre (2), a supposition strongly borne out by his balancer being 3, the number of the combined arts.

The balancer indicating an aspect of a person's work, it would seem here that the combination will mean the musical theatre; and 3 being the number of musical composition, he will probably write music as well as plays. With those three 1s behind it, however, it will be literary music, i.e. not symphonies, but music with words—songs.

The reader will observe how easy these numbers are to interpret. Noel Coward was a genius, and in genius the numbers tend to be exceptionally clear.

Next, his grid:

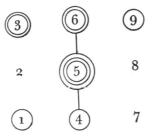

He has the stress line of mastery of material things and affairs, and he will convey an air of mastery ('the Master'), which he did from a very early age—too much so when he was very young; he described himself as an insufferable youth. In ideas, this is the line of materialism; and this being a dramatist, his plays will be materialist in tone—put bluntly, there will be nothing religious about them.

In his work he will be skilled at technique (4), organization (5), and finance (6). It sounds as if he will direct his own plays, and do so with great ability. He has a quick grasp of budgeting (strong 6), and this is further borne out by his having 1 and 9 in balance (when not on a stress line, financial planning).

Stress line 6 to 4 is the classic line of generalship, and

readers of his autobiography, *Present Indicative*, will recall the hair-raising story of setting the Drury Lane stage for *Cavalcade*, his remarkable grasp of how to do it, and the tactics (amounting to generalship) which he used at rehearsals. While this grid is not strong enough to be that of an actual general (nor do the principal numbers apply), this is a person with a remarkable grasp of the practical.

Broad-minded and with wide interests (all the cerebral numbers clothed), he will be as good with personal money as he is with budgeting for the theatre—for the same reasons (strong 6 on stress line, balanced 1 and 9 not on stress line).

His 5 (utterance) is not particularly large. It is more than adequate for a writer, but if he is to use physical utterance as well, it is not quite large enough, though with that desire to please in his birth numbers, he will probably make the most of it. Here it will be remembered that he had not even the beginnings of a singing voice, yet mastered this, and sang inimitably, in his own way.

Absence of 7 on the grid means he is a tireless person (7, the number of laziness), but this carries dangers for a person with a 6 to 4 stress line, representing the human body, the numbers most prone to physical disorders. Having all the numbers of the head (3, 6, 9), the disabilities of 6—physical disorders brought about by over-taxing the nervous system—will not affect him. With tirelessness (lack of 7) in relation to 5 as the larger of the two remaining numbers on the stress line, he is likely to suffer from bouts of exhaustion, due to doing too much.

Being a practical person, he handled this defect (which he knew about) in a clever way, never playing long runs, however successful the show, and indulging, even at the height of his career, in leisurely world travels.

Absence of 7 in a writer or artist also means a person who does not pay much attention to what public opinion (7) may have to say about their work (we saw the same in Callas, in an earlier chapter). The audience will get what the writer wants to give them. If they don't like it, too bad.

Absence of 8 (banking), in a grid with such strong money numbers, means a person who will probably not handle his banking matters personally. This was so of Noel Coward, who from quite an early age relied on a personal business manager.

Absence of 2 and 8, with a good 5, means impatience with people in day-to-day disputations and wranglings; and with 7 also absent (not caring what people think), this feature will be pronounced. In a person who does not achieve success, this can be a great drawback. Noel Coward reached a position where, in this respect, if he gave his views, you listened. If by unwisdom you didn't, there was always the stage door.

The reader will note the curious absence of 2, the number of the theatre. In strong grids this often happens. Many admirals—Lord Mountbatten is a case in point—do not have 8, the number of marine navigation, fleets and navies; while many generals do not have 7, defence. In a person with a clear-cut profession and strong numbers, the presence on the grid of the number typifying the profession can become overpowering, causing disbalance.

In Noel Coward, with a 2 personality and strong numbers of the arts, the additional presence of a 2 on the grid (the musical theatre is anyway represented in a good 3) would become overpowering; and with it would come 2 and 5 with absence of 8 (rule of a civil nature). This, with personality 2, and those arts numbers, would mean that instead of being an artist, he would be arty—a very different matter —probably with a tendency to be feminine and petulant, which was the very last thing Noel Coward was.

The missing 2 on his grid actually means absence of duplicity.

Like quite a few famous men with 2 as their number of personality, though having many women friends, he did not marry.

We will now examine his favourable decades, which are those of his three principal numbers: birth, name, and balancer. These occur bunched together: 1, 2, and 3.

Born in 1899, his first favourable decade occurs in decade 1, starting in 1910, when he is ten years old; and the favourable period will continue for thirty years, through decade 2 and decade 3, lasting until 1939. In 1940 he will enter neutral decades, which will last for the rest of his life.

Had I been a generation older than he, and had he come to me for advice as a boy, saying he wanted to go on the stage, I would have told him of his assets, advising him to think of the theatre first and foremost in terms of writing, because of his 1s, and music, if he developed any talent for it (3). I would then warn him that he must make the utmost use of his time and opportunities when young, his need being to ensure that, by the age of forty, he had established a reputation sufficiently strong to carry him through the rest of his life. If, by the age of thirty-five, he had not made it to success, he must start seriously thinking about getting a safer job, because after forty his chances of success were marginal, and the theatre is the most precarious of professions.

The time to change his occupation, if he was still without prospect of success, would be when he was around thirty-seven or thirty-eight.

This is how the favourable decades work. They begin gently, and increase in strength towards the end. If any change of a radical nature in one's work becomes necessary, and one is faced with a neutral decade ahead, the best moment to make a change is in the last three years of the favourable decade, when it is at its strongest, and when its impetus may be strong enough to carry one through the neutral years which will follow.

People whose favourable decades occur separately, interspersed with neutral ones, need to use their favourable decades to their utmost (isolated ones being weaker than when bunched) to develop impetus to carry them over the neutral years. It is like riding waves. At the right opportunity (the favourable decade), paddle like mad to get and keep on the crest of the wave, and when it breaks (a neutral decade) you can glide gloriously into shore without any effort.

It must be remembered that the longer the favourable period is (maximum, thirty years), the stronger it becomes. So too does the break of the wave, meaning there is greater danger of an upset unless the matter is handled with precision.

Consecutive favourable decades mellow as they go along,

like people in life. Where they occur in a young man, they change from brittle, to fine, to pliable, each strong in its own way.

Where a person is born in a favourable decade, it is usually a good decade wasted, the child being too young to make any use of it.

Where, as with Noel Coward, a favourable decade begins at the age of ten, it indicates a person liable to grow up quickly, in respect of ideas, inclinations, or ambition, and wish to have a job as soon as possible. In Coward's life this process was exceptionally fast, due to being by birth (directional sense) a 1, the number which knows what it wants to do, and does it.

His mind set on the theatre, and with his mother's encouragement, he made his first appearance at ten. By fourteen he was on the professional stage in London; and by nineteen, people in the profession knew about him.

However brilliant, one is too young to make full use of a favourable decade at this age. One is struggling to master self-expression. In the mellowing of these three consecutive decades, this first one can be largely ruled out; he simply started young, and gained experience. His brittle decade came in the 1920s, his fine one in the 1930s, and he did not have the pliable one. In the 1920s, in fact, he personified the brittle young man.

Once in his 2 decade (the number of his name, the most important), things moved fast. At the age of twenty-two he had his first play on at the Savoy Theatre. After his first success, *The Vortex*, he became the most talked of person in London, whether as an object of admiration or dismay. By the end of the decade, with the triumphant success of *Bitter-Sweet* in London and New York, he was an international name.

The year after he entered his third decade (more mellow —in his case, the fine decade), he signalized the fact with the epic *Cavalcade* (1931). Overnight, he ceased to be the brittle young man, and became a national figure.

He then proceeded to produce his most finished and accomplished works: the best revue he ever wrote, *Words and Music*, his masterpiece in the musical theatre, *Conver-*

sation Piece, and the changeable bill of short plays com-
positely known as *To-Night at 8.30*, which demonstrate the
most consummate skill in a playwright. Were it possible to
teach playwriting—which it isn't—*To-Night at 8.30* would
be a textbook. As an example, *Hands Across the Sea*: how
to write a play about absolutely nothing, and keep an
audience shaking with laughter from start to finish.

To the same decade belong two of his best comedies,
Present Laughter and *Blithe Spirit*, though due to war
conditions these were not performed till the early forties
(neutral times). This is something which frequently happens. One reaps in a neutral decade the fruits of work done
in a favourable one. A person's best work, which satisfies
him most, is usually done in a favourable decade.

By the end of the thirties, Noel Coward was the most
prestigious name in dramatic art. The only person comparable with him on the same kind of platform was Sacha
Guitry. He had made it to forty, with reputation enough to
carry him through more than one lifetime.

Though he kept that position for the rest of his life, from
1940 onwards, when he entered neutral decades, he was in
fact living on reputation. His best work was done. Only once
after that date, with the comedy *Nude With Violin*, did he
touch again the high pitch of his work as a young man.

Moreover, those later decades really *were* neutral to him.
After the war, the age which he personified had gone. People
went to see a Noel Coward show in hope of a sentimental
reminder of happier days lost; his audiences were no longer
as young as they used to be.

His work had always been presented by the foremost
managements of the day. After the war he decided to finance
his own shows. A series of costly failures followed, in which
he lost a great deal of money. He recouped this handsomely;
but during his later years he had to work much harder than
would ordinarily be expected in a man of such achievement.

By comparison with Bernard Shaw, for example.

Entering into management, in a person who has not done
it before, ranks as a major new departure, or change. It is
unwise to undertake such in a neutral decade. It is unlikely
to succeed, as Coward's experience shows.

As a final touch, let me bring in the fourth digit of the year.

In a favourable decade, there are particular moments when the last two digits of the year (the digits must be taken together) make up one or other of our principal numbers. In a person with isolated numbers, these moments do not have much effect; a year is soon gone. But in bunched numbers they do have effect, and in Noel Coward's life the bunched numbers came at the end of the decade, the strongest part of it.*

In addition, they overlapped the next decade, giving still further strength.

The first series occurred in years 19, 20, and 21 (1919–1921), when, though very active, he was still too young to benefit much from them. The next series occurred in years 28, 29, and 30 (1, 2, and 3).

Here he was of an age for these years to be of real importance, occurring at the end of a decade, and running over into the next one, also favourable. This is a moment when one might expect to find particular achievement, success, or (in the case of a man with a routine career) a sense of ease, and of things going right.

1928, the first in this series, was the year of the revue *This Year of Grace,* which epitomized an age and identified Noel Coward for ever as the interpreter of his time.

1929 was the year of *Bitter-Sweet,* the music of which swept the world and gave him international fame.

1930 was the year of the masterpiece among all his comedies, *Private Lives.*

Those are, in fact, the three crucial works in Noel Coward's life, and they occur in the three crucial years.

* Another year to keep an eye on is when any one of a person's three principal numbers repeats itself, viz. 1922, 1933, 1944 etc. Such years are liable to be of significance.

2

On a Lioness

There was once a girl called

RUTH ELIZABETH DAVIS
9 3 2 8   5 3 9 8 1 2 5 2 8   4 1 4 9 1
   4   8   1
                    4

Date of birth:

5 April 1908
5   4   9
    9   Balancer (4 + 9): 4

By birth she is 9, the number of sheer power which is not intrinsically attached to anything. Observe that it is made up of another 9, together with 5 plus 4 directly repeating her date (i.e. the date is not 23 April, but actually 5 and 4), which makes a third 9. This is a very powerful number indeed, a triple 9, almost more than a man could cope with, but wonderful for a woman, provided she finds her *métier*.

9 by birth means that name and balancer will be the same, meaning close identification between personality and work. By name and balancer she is 4, the woman's number of the fundamental, the universal. With that triple 9 by birth, this is a little girl who will see herself from the start in terms of the world—tiresome, but inescapable.

In terms of what kind of life will she see herself? To answer this, we need the grid.

Normally, this being an unmarried girl, I would first do the grid with her personal name only. But she herself was

not satisfied with her name, feeling it was not quite *her*, so
to do this will be a waste of time. At home she was called
Pinky, but nicknames are inadmissible in numerology. Let
us therefore set the grid with her full name:

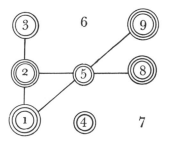

She will want a career (stress line 1 to 9), and will not
be easy to marry. Her 1 and 9 are evenly balanced on a stress
line, meaning that, though probably conveying outwardly a
sense of great confidence (triple 9 by birth), inwardly she is
unsure of herself in a woman's way—unsure of herself as a
woman, given to doubt, and questioning her own motives.

She has the line of dedication to a career, or talent—line
1 to 3, weighted in 1, ideas. This, however, is not a writer.
That strong 2 (the theatre, a social person) means a life
which is too *mouvementée* for a writer. This is not a
tranquil grid.

She has the line of service to others (2 to 8), which is very
strong, with balance at both ends, indicating great command
in the expression and control of the emotions. This being
the line of the organizer of people, she is a capable person.
Were she to make a career in business, which with that
strong 8 (woman's number of commerce) she could, she
would need a woman partner (absence of 6, the woman's
number of banking); and being 4 by name and balancer (4,
the universal, and a masterful woman), she would have
difficulty in finding and keeping a business partner. This
stress line is therefore more likely to be concerned with
emotional expression.

This being so, the stress line 1 to 3 will mean dedication
to a talent; and with that strong 2 (the theatre) coinciding

with a strong line of emotional control and expression (line 2 to 8), this is going to be an actress.

Absence of 7, with 1 and 4 clothed: she will be tireless, and will not care much what people think of her.

Furthermore, with the tremendous power and drive of her triple 9 (number of birth, directional sense), coupled with 4 by name and balancer (4, the universal), to become a star will not be enough. She will be a queen of stars, *the* star, come hell or high water—a humiliating state of affairs when it comes to giving one's first audition. She will detest auditions.

We will now float down from the pinnacle of the Empire State Building (Ruth Elizabeth's mental habitat) to street level—Broadway is a short walk.

With her strong directional sense, allied to talent, at an early age this young lady decided to become a star—I repeat, a star, not an actress. And the first thing she resolved upon was to do something about her name, which was not quite *her*. So she changed it to

BETTE DAVIS

2 5 2 2 5 4 1 4 9 1

7   1

8   Balancer (8 + 9): 8

She now had the two most powerful numbers on the board (9 and 8). As well, Bette being a 7, she had given herself the third power number, the negative one, bringing femininity to numbers which would otherwise be too formidably masculine for a woman to carry easily.

Formidable, however, is the word for these numbers, owing to the power of triple 9.

8, the woman's number of commerce, is the ideal number of career for a woman who is engaged in any of the activities with which women are concerned. In an actress, it means a thoroughly business-like person, who wants contracts (8, woman's number of law) to be cut and dried, and cannot stand any form of muddle. To others she conveys an air of being business-like. She is reliable, and very consistent in quality of performance.

Her grid now changed to this:

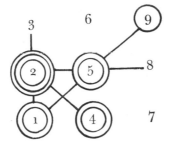

Her numbers have become more concentrated. Her number of the theatre (2) is the strongest (the only one to reach three rings). She has the line of service to others (2 to 8), which we saw in her case meant emotional control and expression (the heart line). Though she has lost her 8, this is compensated for by her two powerful 8s of name and balancer. With another 8 on the grid, it would become overpowering, and cause disbalance.

She still has her worldly success line (1 to 9), and she has lost that doubting balance of 1 and 9 on stress line. With this name, she is set to go, sure of herself.

She has the line 3 to 1, weighted in 1, dedication to a talent. She had that anyway, but it has now been concentrated on a woman's intellectual expression (2 and 1), with powerful crosses all over the place. This, in fact, is a grid which, in a woman, is about one centimetre from the humanly uncontrollable. In an actress, it is liable to mean a presentation of the unparalleled; in almost anyone else, grave instability. 2 and 1 are the two most sensitive numbers of all, and they cannot take much in the way of crosses.

She has literary sense (good 1 on stress line), and will be a good judge of a script. Note 4 and 5 balanced on the central vertical line: as an actress she will be strong on technique (4).

Stress line 2 to 4: she is a perfectionist—2, the heart in air (desire) seeking meticulous detail (4).

She has only one cerebral number (9), but this deficiency only matters with women who have to exercise authority over others in their work, and she doesn't have to.

She remains tireless (absence of 7) and is not swayed by what critics (7) say about her, whether good or bad.

Her work in the theatre will have nothing to do with music (absence of 3). She once sang a song—*They're either too young or too old*. It lives in memory by being unique in her career.

Absence of 6 (woman's number of banking) and 8, even though the latter is on a stress line, and is one of her principal numbers, in double: though extremely practical and sensible about money matters, she will probably feel more at ease with someone else to add advice to her own wishes, and deal with such matters for her.

Acute-angle cross over 5 (the mouth): acting apart, she will not care for making public appearances, and be unlikely to accept speaking engagements.

A woman with stress line 1 to 9 is, at best, difficult to marry, if she fulfils her wish to have a career. For her, work comes first, and home life is an adjunct, as in a man.

Greta Garbo, the only screen actress comparable with Bette Davis, also has this stress line; and it is her only one, as with Sarah Bernhardt. Garbo wisely steered clear of marriage, which in a career woman with this stress line is usually the soundest course in the long run—unless a quite exceptional husband presents himself.

With Bette Davis, this (at best of times) difficult situation is rendered infinitely more complex by the line 1 to 9 occurring with stress line 2 to 4, one of the meanings of which, when the line is weighted in 2 (as it is), is a longing for a happy, normal home life. In simple terms, this line means passionate desire (2, heart in air) to cook (4), cooking here representing the very fundamental (4) of home.

This line, in a woman, when in conjunction with stress line 1 to 9, becomes a line of marital disaster. Homely desire (2 to 4, weighted in 2) is working against reality, which is a life spent making it to the top (line 1 to 9) and dedication to a talent (line 1 to 3). Marriage in these conditions cannot endure, except where two people are forced to stay together because of financial circumstances—in particular, that unless together, there is not enough money to look after children—and then it is likely to be a marriage of misery.

To make it even more difficult, Bette Davis has the stress line of service to others (2 to 8), heavily weighted in 2, meaning a *desire* to serve, as a woman serves her husband and home. The total of this grid, seen in this aspect, is a numerical presentation of the impossible.

The theme of her autobiography, *The Lonely Life*, is this deep desire for home and her inability to attain it. Four times she has entered into marriage, and each time it has broken up, because she was striving (2, desire) to achieve the impossible. Colossal but transitory emotional affairs (Sarah Bernhardt, Mrs. Patrick Campbell) were not for her. She desired marriage and a home (stress line 2 to 4). As one of her girlhood friends said:

'Bette, you could be the bee's knees if you wouldn't take life so seriously.'

In a way which puritans would not agree with, the friend was right. Bette Davis' children, however, will reflect with admiration that their mother did not take the hint.

Stress line 2 to 4, though it need not be, nearly always turns out to be a line of real personal difficulty. In a man, it tends to the criminal (2, duplicity, 4, technique), in a woman to the neurotic (2, emotion, 4, neurosis). Bette Davis is a wonderful example of a person who converted this difficult line into an attribute. No screen actress has ever compared with her in portraying the neurotic.

Her greatest triumph in this respect was as 'Aunt' Charlotte in *Now, Voyager*. Without anything overt by gesture or word, the sense of submerged neurosis which she sustained from beginning to end of that picture—she seethed with neurosis, while seeming perfectly natural— has never been portrayed with such extraordinary truth. Anyone who has real-life dealings with the psychotic knows that outwardly they seem completely normal. But what actress, save one, has ever been able to convey this?

The Lonely Life, incidentally, is about the best auto-biography ever written by an actress (1, literary sense, with strong 2, sometimes a woman's number of literature, combined with managerial, feminine 8).

Had this lady remained Ruth Elizabeth Davis, her marital problems would not have occurred. With her sense of unsureness as a woman (balanced 1 and 9 on stress line), I doubt if she would have married at all. Self-doubt would have held her back. But that name, while being determined to be *the* star, might not have made it. There is a certain ordinariness about the grid, which is not quite right for *the* star.

Now, to favourable decades.

Had she remained Ruth Elizabeth Davis, she would have had a favourable decade in the 1940s, and a strong one, being 4 twice, by name and balancer. As it was, by changing her name, she deprived herself of a favourable decade till 1980, when she will be seventy-two. Throughout the prime of life, she has no favourable decade.

This, in a little girl who had decided to be *the* star, means that every inch of her life will be struggle, if not (triple 9 by birth) a fight. Not surprisingly, her autobiography opens with these words:

'I have always been driven by some distant music—a battle hymn no doubt—for I have been at war from the beginning.' *

And thus it was: a fight to prevent herself being made into Hollywood's idea of a glamour girl; a fight to keep the name Bette Davis; a fight to get intelligent parts; a fight for realism, as opposed to prettiness and insipidity; a fight to be allowed to be herself.

Only once in the long career of the greatest actress of the screen has anything fallen into her lap, and then she nearly missed it.

This was when George Arliss telephoned to offer her what was to be her first star part, the female lead opposite him in *The Silent Voice*, or as it was known in the United States, *The Man Who Played God*.

Arliss was the uncrowned king of movies. Thinking it was a hoaxer, when he gave his name, she replied in her haughtiest English accent:

'Of course, and how are you, old boy?'

She made it, of course. Triple nines do.

In a person with no favourable decades, one ignores the

---

* It is fascinating that the first verb she uses in her book should be 'drive' —the exact meaning of a triple 9.

decade digit of the year, and concentrates on the fourth digit, and the fourth digit *only*.

Here numerology becomes precarious. It is a form of knowledge which must not be pressed to extremes.

In a person with isolated numbers, the occurrence of one of them in the fourth digit of the year usually means little or nothing. Where numbers are bunched—as in Bette Davis' 8 and 9—there is just a chance they may be of influence.

These numbers first hit the century for her in 1928 and 1929, when, aged twenty and twenty-one, she was a struggling young actress in New York. Not being the pussie type, she was the wrong age for the numbers.

The second time they occurred was in 1938 and 1939. Turning to her book, one finds the proud words—the grandest an actress can say:

'In the year 1939 I secured my career and my stardom forever.'

It was the year in which she appeared in five movies, all of them successful, and for the second time—this time feeling she merited it, which on the first occasion she did not—won the Academy Award. It was also the year of two of her most admired pictures: *Dark Victory* and *The Old Maid*.

In 1980—favourable decades begin gently—Bette Davis will enter the first favourable decade of her life. If she keeps her health, it may well be that her most satisfying and rewarding work still lies ahead.

As one of her many admirers, I hope it will be so.

But if it is, let directors be prepared. She once played Queen Elizabeth I. After 1980 she may not just be playing. . . .

3
On a Tiger

A striking example of favourable decades in later life is Georges Clémenceau, born on 28 September 1841.

By name a 5, and by birth a 6, his favourable decades occurred between 1850, when he was only nine years old, and 1869. This meant he made an early start, and had a brittle decade in his twenties. These years established him, leading to the unforgettable moments when he was Mayor of Montmartre during the Siege of Paris. But being fundamentally a statesman, these decades came to him too young.

In 1870, itself a year of disaster for France, he entered neutral decades. The rest of his life was one long struggle, *sans relâche*, culminating in steering his country through the final horror of the Great War, and the difficult treaty that followed. When, in 1920, as Premier, he and his cabinet resigned, it looked as if it was the end of him. A new era had begun, which would have no time for a man of his age.

In that year, however, he entered his third favourable decade. By balancer he was a 2.

On the day of his cabinet's resignation, who could have believed what the next years held for him? Relaxed and at ease (the essence of a favourable decade), he toured the world in a leisurely way, lectured and wrote. From the smaller world of Paris politics, he moved into an international arena of glory, recognized as the greatest statesman of the age, a man whose chancest word, in whatever country, was remembered. Wherever he went, streets and squares were named after him. To this day, the presence of his name denotes the route of his travels.

Far from being ended in 1920, he entered glory, and he died at the pinnacle of it, in 1929, just escaping the tiresomeness of the neutral decade which lay before him, which, being too old, he would have found boring.

IV
BUT, A WORD FROM THE JANITOR

By drawing attention to a life with no favourable decades in the prime of life—that of Bette Davis—I have brought the interpretation of numbers in the digits of the year to about as far as I think they will go.

We all of us know how there is a particular time of year, sometimes even to the day, at which decisive events or changes in our lives are apt to occur. By experience, we each discover for ourselves this time, or exact date.

The date is nearly always fortunate, though we may not instantly see it thus. It usually reflects one of our three principal numbers.

If a person has such a date, it is impossible to determine in which years it will be operative, in which years neutral. It is equally impossible to tell, in an infant's numbers, which day of the year this peculiar day will be, if there is to be one. If anyone has one, by the age of thirty he will normally have discovered it.

Similarly, when doing the numbers of a youth, it is not possible to predict with certainty what career he will have. From the character reading one can see clearly enough what type of occupation he will be suited to, but whether or not he will find his way into it is another matter. Where numbers indicate exceptional talent and bent—we observed this in Noel Coward—it is of course possible to predict with reasonable certainty that one's prediction will come true; but this is uncommon and numbers on their face value are frequently misleading.

As an example, one may have a man who is a 6 by name and whose general numbers suggest the law or commerce, yet who is in fact an actor. Inquire closely, however, and it may be found that the actor is regularly engaged to play the parts of lawyers or businessmen, because this is the type of personality he conveys. Equally, one may find a person with the numbers of a wise statesman, yet who is in fact a village policeman. Yet inquire deeper and it may be found that he has a statesmanlike approach to the problems of his village, and is in fact exercising this ability in his own way.

Provided it is borne in mind that the numerals represent character, not circumstance, and that prediction on the basis of them is little more than friendly advice, numerology will not let you down. Indeed, if you become adept at it, you will discover that the accuracy of numbers can be embarrassing.

This is as far as numerology will go.

Lucky numbers, for which mankind has an incorrigible affection, have nothing to do with this subject. They perhaps exist. If they do, I have never succeeded in identifying them.

As for lucky months, lucky days, and lucky hours—there is a numerologist in India who makes a speciality of lucky hours for doing things—I must frankly say that, if anyone becomes as concentrated as this on the subject, the likelihood is they need to consult a mental specialist, not a numerologist.

The lucky hour at which to telephone the object of your affections is when she is in.

Or out, if you have the number.

INDEX